ORBIS MUSICAE

CONTENTS

The Music and Text of the Falasha Sabbath	*Kay Kaufman Shelemay*	3
Divergency of Theory and Practice in Japanese Buddhist Chant	*Janos Kárpáti*	23
Toward Comparative Study of Persian Radifs: Focus on Dastgāh–E Māhour	*Bruno Nettl and Daryoosh Shenassa*	29
The Four Styles of Notre-Dame Organa	*Hans Tischler*	44
The Glee: the Term and its Connotation – An Annotated Documentation	*Herzl Shmueli*	54
Invention Individuelle et Tradition Collective dans la Musique Juive de Hongrie	*Judit Frigyesi*	71
Childbirth Songs among Sephardic Jews of Balkan Origin	*Susana Weich-Shahak*	87
Research Reports:		
The Nāy or Arab Flute	*Yohanan Ron*	104
Robert Schumann's Concept of Music Education	*Lia Laor*	109
Musimple: Computer-Based Learning of 7-Sign Music Notation System	*Yael Bukspan*	111
From the Bookshelf	*Hanoch Avenary*	114

ASSAPH: Studies in the Arts

Published by the Faculty of Visual and Performing Arts,

Tel-Aviv University

Section A: ORBIS MUSICAE, Studies in Musicology

ISSN 0303-3937

Editorial Board: Eric Werner, Edith Gerson-Kiwi, Hanoch Avenary,

Herzl Shmueli, Judith Cohen, David Bloch

In charge of this issue:

David Bloch

© 1983 by Department of Musicology, Tel-Aviv University

Any reproduction of the articles published in ORBIS MUSICAE
without the editor's written consent is prohibited.

Phototypesetting by "Machshev-Ot" – M. Rachlin Ltd.

The Music and Text of the Falasha Sabbath

Kay Kaufman Shelemay, *New York*

Although the Falashas are thought to be an indigenous Ethiopian people who acquired Jewish traditions at some point in their history, both the date and the source (or sources) of these Jewish traditions are still debated.[1] Most Falashas live in northwestern Ethiopia where they have been known for centuries as metalurgists and potters. Although they share material culture as well as spoken and liturgical languages with their Ethiopian Christian neighbors,[2] the marked Judaic content of their religious life has attracted the attention of outsiders.[3]

The Falasha religious life, preserved by an active clergy against outside pressures for centuries, is fast changing to accommodate their relatively late incorporation into the Jewish mainstream. Western Jews made their first sustained contact with the Falashas in the mid-nineteenth century and, since the early twentieth century, many Falashas have learned Hebrew language and liturgy. In 1973, the Falashas were recognized as Jews by the Sephardic Rabbi and today a growing Falasha community is found in Israel.[4]

The current Falasha clergy is comprised of priests (*qes* or *kahen*) who were

---

1. Falashas, along with other Ethiopians, claim descent from Menelik, fabled son of King Solomon and the Queen of Sheba. Scholars have suggested that Ethiopians may have received Jewish traditions from Southern Arabian or Egyptian Jews. For discussion of various theories, see Robert L. Hess, "Toward a History of the Falasha," *Eastern African History,* ed. by Daniel F. McCall and others. Boston University Papers on Africa, vol. 3. (New York: Frederick A. Praeger, 1969), 107-132, and Wolf Leslau, *The Falasha Anthology* (New York: Schocken Books, 1969). My own research indicates that the impact of Judaized Ethiopian monastic groups upon the Falashas has been underestimated. See Shelemay, "Historical Ethnomusicology: Reconstructing Falasha Liturgical History," *Ethnomusicology* XXIV (May, 1980), 233-258.
2. Falashas used to speak their own Agau dialect until Amharic, the national Ethiopian language, entered their area. The Falasha liturgy is in Geez, an ancient Semitic language used within the Ethiopian Church. Phrases in Agau are also found in Falasha liturgy. There is no evidence the Falashas knew Hebrew before the modern period. See Wolf Leslau, "A Falasha Religious Dispute, Excursus 3, "Did the Falashas Speak Hebrew?," *Proceedings of the American Academy for Jewish Research* 16 (1947), 89-94.
3. Falasha observance of the Sabbath, male circumcision on the eighth day and dietary laws are usually cited as prominent Jewish elements in their tradition; all are shared by Ethopian Christians as well. See Edward Ullendorff, *Ethiopia and the Bible* (London: Oxford Univ. Press, 1968) and Ephraim Isaac, "An Obscure Component in Ethiopian Church History," *Le Muséon* LXXXV, 1-2 (1972), 225-258. More striking are the parallels between Falasha and Jewish calendars, including Falasha celebration of holidays similar or equivalent to Passover (*fasika*), Yom Kippur (*'astasrēyo*), and Sukkot (*ba'āla masallat*).

once part of a larger clerical order that included Falasha monks and nuns.[5] Falasha priests still transmit their liturgy as an oral tradition, accompanying their performances in village prayerhouses with a drum (*nagārit*) and gong (*qačel*).

The music and text of the Falasha Sabbath (*sanbat*) are our subject here.[6] An examination of these materials provides insight into aspects of Falasha musical/liturgical practice. Falasha priests today are unable to discuss the musical content of their liturgy in detail; therefore, an investigation of music and text of a single liturgical occasion is a necessary and useful procedure through which we can both test surviving exegesis and better define parameters of musical/liturgical practice.

The Falasha Sabbath in its Ethiopian Context

The Sabbath has always been at the center of Jewish religious practice. For the Falashas, the Sabbath has been additionally a critical factor in both their own and others' definitions of their religious identity. The importance of the Sabbath within Falasha religious life is reflected in the network of customs surrounding its observance:

> The Falasha women start their preparations for the Sabbath on Friday afternoon. They wash both their bodies and their clothing in the river and then begin to prepare the beer, grind the grain, and bake the bread. The men cease their work at midday and also wash. After sunset the fires in the houses are extinguished ... No intercourse with women is allowed on that night .... No drum is beaten and no gong is sounded during the Sabbath prayers. No work of any kind is done on the Sabbath; no water is drawn at the river, no fire is lit to prepare food, no coffee is boiled... only cold food and drink are used on this day... The Falashas are not supposed to leave the confines of their village on the Sabbath. They may not quarrel on this day, and the usual salutation is *sanbat salam, sanbat salam,* "Sabbath peace, Sabbath peace."[7]

4. Jacques Faitlovitch began a school for Falasha children in Addis Ababa during 1924. By 1956, thirty-three schools sponsored by Jewish organizations had opened in Falasha villages. *Cf.* Yona Bogale, "The Beta Israel (Falasha) Schools," n.d. (mimeographed). A recent discussion of Falasha recognition by the Israeli Rabbinate and immigration to Israel is found in Louis Rappaport, *The Lost Jews* (New York: Stein and Day, 1980).
5. The Falashas adopted a monastic order from Ethiopian Christian monks during the fourteenth and fifteenth centuries. See Hess, "Toward a History," 112-113.
6. This article is based upon data gathered in Ethiopia during 1973-1975. The liturgical examples discussed here are transcribed from field tapes of the prayerhouse liturgy performed in Ambober, Begemder and Semien Province. A key to the system of textual transliteration and musical symbols is found in Appendix 1.

Most of these traditions were still observed in 1973. One striking change was the performance of a Hebrew prayer service by young Falashas after the traditional Geez ritual on Sabbath morning. Other observers wrote of Sabbath customs that have not survived this century. The nineteenth-century missionary Flad described a communal meal held after the conclusion of Falasha Sabbath worship:

> After the conclusion of the ceremonies attending divine worship, bread and pepper-soup, together with sour milk, are brought into the Mesgeed (Note: *Mesgid* was the name of the Falasha prayerhouse, today called *ṣelot bēt*, literally "prayer house") by all who can afford it... This feast is called Makfalt or Jaendshera Maswaot (bread sacrifice). Beer is afterwards drunk... When all are satisfied, if circumstances permit, a portion of the law is read...[8]

Today, Falasha priests conduct a brief service about one-half hour long after sunset on Sabbath eve, and a ritual of several hours beginning before dawn on Sabbath morning. Every seventh Sabbath is celebrated as *yasanbat sanbat* (Sabbath of Sabbaths).[9] Priests from surrounding villages meet in a central prayerhouse. After the brief evening ritual, they rest and eat dinner. They begin a vigil around 10 p.m., pausing in early morning hours to drink *ṭella* (local beer), a tradition reminiscent of the communal meal described by Flad. The ritual then resumes until 9 a.m. During a break lasting until after noon, Hebrew-speaking Falashas perform the Hebrew Sabbath liturgy. After again singing Geez prayers from 1 to 4 p.m., the priests adjourn to a local home for *ṭella*. Around sunset, they return to the prayerhouse to complete the ritual, accompanying their prayers with dancing.

Falasha Sabbath observance almost certainly emerges from the complex and controversial history of the Sabbath in Ethiopia. Ethiopian Christians have observed the Saturday Sabbath through their history. Attempts to shift Ethiopian Christian Sabbath observance to Sunday during the fourteenth and fifteenth centuries resulted in a conflict and schism resolved only through

---

7. Leslau, *Falasha Anthology*, xxxii-xxxiii. Leslau's description is based upon a 1947 visit to Falasha villages, including Ambober.
8. Johann M. Flad, *Falashas of Abyssinia*, trans. by S.P. Goodhart (London: William Macintosh, 1869), 45. An allusion to this ceremony is found in the homily at the end of the *sanbat* morning ritual, which begins with the statement "Now the sacrifice (*masawā'ot*) and honor to the Lord."
9. Although Falashas now call this holiday by the Amharic *yasanbat sanbat*, it is known as *zabarabu sanbat* in Geez, or *langato* in Agau. There was evidently an annual *yasanbat sanbat* in the past, but Falashas are now confused about its date. See Leslau, *Falasha Anthology*, 31.

legitimation of both Saturday and Sunday Sabbaths.[10] Among the Judaic traditions surviving in Ethiopian Christianity, Saturday Sabbath observance has been the most persistently controversial.

Another aspect of Falasha Sabbath observance shared with Ethiopian Christians is the personification of the Sabbath,[11] found both in Falasha literary works and in the Sabbath liturgy. Falashas view the Sabbath as a female figure personifying the heavenly world.[12] The Sabbath is described in one Falasha literary work, Te'ezaza Sanbat (The Commandments of the Sabbath), as interceding with God on behalf of sinners, descending to Sheol to deliver wrong-doers, and being crowned by angels.[13]

Therefore, we find a Falasha Sabbath observance which is strict in ritual, rich in imagery, and closely tied to precedents within Ethiopian Church history. We will examine below the prayers and music of the Sabbath ritual. The Sabbath of Sabbaths, which contains the major prayers cited here as well as others held in common with another Falasha vigil, will not be discussed in detail.

The Texts

Falasha Sabbath rituals share most of their textual content with other occasions in the Falasha liturgical cycle. Figure 1 sets forth the major prayers of Sabbath eve and morning, named, as in Falasha practice, by their textual incipits.

The Sabbath liturgy contains a nucleus of prayers which are found in most other Falasha liturgical orders. (See Figure 2) These prayers, evidently statutory to Falasha prayerhouse worship, are said by Falasha priests to have been part of the Falasha Monastic Office.[14]

10. Several groups of Ethiopian Christian monks were excommunicated for their refusal to forfeit Saturday Sabbath observance during these disputes. While in exile, they established monasteries among Ethiopians in outlying areas of the empire, including among the Falashas. For discussion of this controversy, see Taddesse Tamrat, *Church and State in Ethiopia* (Oxford: At the Clarendon Press, 1972), 196-220, and Taddesse Tamrat, "Some Notes on the Fifteenth Century Stephanite 'Heresy' in the Ethiopian Church," *Rassegna di studi Etiopici* 22 (1966), 103-115. These Judaic monastic groups, termed Jewish-Christians by Ephraim Isaac, were anti-Trinitarians who refused to worship Mary or prostrate themselves to the Cross and insisted upon adhering to Biblical precepts and worshipping one God. See Ephraim Isaac, *A New Text-Critical Introduction to Mashafa Berhān, With a Translation of Book I* (Leiden: E.J. Brill, 1973) and Ephraim Isaac, "An Obscure Component in Ethiopian Church History."
11. One of the Ethiopian anaphoras contains a song welcoming the Sabbath Queen. See Ernst Hammerschmidt, *Stellung und Bedeutung des Sabbats in Äthiopien* (Stuttgart: W. Kohlhammer Verlag, 1963), 63.
12. Leslau, *Falasha Anthology*, 3.
13. Leslau, *Falasha Anthology*, 3-39.

Figure 1: *Sanbat* order of service

Key to Figure 1:
*   Prayers performed also on *yasanbat sanbat, seged,* and *ʾastasrēyo.*
**   Prayers performed only on *sanbat* and *yasanbat sanbat.*
No asterisk   Statutory prayers occurring in following rituals:
   BS – *berhān saraqa* (the light appeared)
   BM – *baʿāla maṣallat* (feast of tabernacles)
   A – *ʾastasrēyo* (atonement)
   S – *seged* (to bow)
   SS – *yasanbat sanbat* (Sabbath of Sabbaths)
   D – daily
   /AM – morning ritual only
   #1, etc. repetition of same prayer

Sanbat eve
** *ʾadonāy* (Adonay)
   yetbārak (blessed)
      BS,BM,A,S,SS,D
** *bārek sanbateye* (bless my Sabbath)
   qeddus (holy)
      BS,BM,A,S,SS,D
   Agau prayer

               Sanbat morning
                * *negus ʾanta* (You are king)
                  semeʿānna ʾegziʾo #1 (Hear us, Lord)
                     BS,BM,A,S,SS,D/ AM
                  kalhu kwellu malāʾekt (all the angels cried)
                     BS,BM,A,S,SS,D/AM
                  semeʿānna ʾegziʾo #2
                ** *waradat sanbat* (Sabbath descended)
                ** *watebēlo sanbat* (and Sabbath said)
                  semeʿānna ʾegziʾo #3
                ** *negus ʾadonāy* (King, Adonay)
                  semeʿānna ʾegziʾo #4
                  genāyu laʾegziʾabḥēr (submit to the Lord)
                     BS,BM,A,S,SS,D/AM
                * *yetbārak* (Daniel 3) (blessed)
                * *neʿu nesged* (come and bow)
                * *ʾesēbḥo laʾegziʾabḥēr* (I will praise the Lord)
                ** *semāʿe ʾesrāʾēl* (Hear, Israel)
                  yetbārak #1 (blessed)
                     BS,BM,A,S,SS,D
                * *amlākeya* (my God)

qeddus (holy)
    BS,BM,A,S,SS,D
yetbārak #2 (blessed)
Homily about *sanbat*
Closing formula (There is no other God forever. We believe in one God. (twice) Peace.)

Figure 2: Statutory Prayers in *sanbat* ritual

Textual Incipit   *Time(s)*   *Musical Incipit*

yetbārak (blessed) sunset / morning
Evening version and #2 share text;
#1 recurs after major prayers
in many Falasha rituals and contains
text partially resembling Jewish
half *qaddiš*[1]

qeddus (holy)   afternoon/
     or with *yetbārak*

Shares text with Jewish *qeddušá* and
Christian *trisagion*

kalhu kwellu malā'ekt before
(all the angels cried) dawn
Shares text with *qeddus;* describes
angels in seven heavens of God
genāyu la'egzi'abḥēr before dawn
(submit to the Lord)
Partially drawn from Psalm 136
seme'ānna 'egzi'o   before dawn/
(hear us Lord)   sunrise

Fig. 2 (continued)

(hear us Lord)

<hr />

[1] For further discussion of relationship between Falasha prayers and Jewish liturgical models, see Kay K. Shelemay, "A Comparative Study: Jewish Liturgical Forms in the Falasha Liturgy?", *Yuval, Studies of the Jewish Music Research Centre V*, forthcoming.

<hr />

A second group of prayers for Sabbath are also found in other Falasha rituals, although without the regularity of the statutory prayers. The *yetbārak* (Canticle of the Three Youths in the Fire from Daniel 3, apocryphal), *ne'u nesged*, and *'esebḥo* occur also on the pilgrimage festival *seged* and the fast *'astasrēyo*. The prayers *negus 'anta* and *'amlākeya* are performed during the vigil for the fast *'astasrēyo*. (See Figure 3)

Prayers performed only on Sabbath (and the Sabbath of Sabbaths) comprise a relatively small portion of the liturgy. For the eve, these prayers are *'adonāy* and *bārek sanbateye*. Four prayers are performed only on Sabbath morning: *waradat sanbat*, *watebēlo sanbat*, *negus 'adonāy*, and *semā'e 'esrā'ēl*. Transcriptions and partial texts of these prayers are provided in Appendix 1.

Despite their similar textual incipits, the *'adonāy* and *negus 'adonāy* do not share textual content. However, similar textual motifs, incorporating images of the personified Sabbath, link the *bārek sanbateye*, *waradat sanbat*, and *watebēlo sanbat*. All three prayers draw upon texts or ideas expressed in the Falasha literary work *Te'ezaza Sanbat*, providing evidence of interaction between Falasha literature and the oral liturgical tradition. Within *bārek sanbateye* and *watebēlo sanbat*, Sabbath mediates between man and God.[15] Verses of *waradat sanbat* describe the Sabbath's descent from heaven to earth, including to Jerusalem, where she is crowned by angels.[16]

14. Falasha priests in 1973 were able to perform portions of the Falasha monastic Office, said seven times daily until the death of the last Falasha monk in their area in the late 1960's.
15. A nineteenth-century source reports a Falasha comment that "Mary is the mediator of the Christians, the Sabbath is ours." Philoxene Luzzatto, "Mémoire sur les Juifs d'Abyssinie ou Falashas," *Archives Israelites*, 13 (1852), 345. The refrain "I am alive" in *bārek sanbateye* also derives from *Te'ezaza Sanbat:* "Holy and praised is the Lord of Sabaoth. He is living." Leslau, *Falasha Anthology*, 25.
16. See Leslau, *Falasha Anthology*, 36.

Figure 3: Prayers shared by *sanbat, yasanbat sanbat, seged, 'astasrēyo*

Textual Incipit and Summary   *Musical Incipit*

negus 'anta (you are king alone, before everything)
Texts of praise and intercession;
Agau texts; total 19 verses

yetbārak (text from Daniel 3, apoc.)
(Blessed be the Lord ... who is worthy of praise)
Canticle text with interpolations;[1]
total 9 verses

ne'u nesged (come and bow and worship him alone)
Possible source: Psalm 95: 6-7;
Texts of praise and intercession;
total 27 verses

'esēbho (I will praise the Lord while I live)
Probable source: Psalm 146:1;
additional texts; total 5 verses, then irregular; may be composite prayer

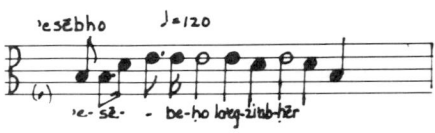

'amlākeya (My God, my God, I come to you and my lips praise you)
Possible source: Psalm 63:3;
additional verses from Psalm 150;
total 5 verses, then irregular;
may be composite prayer; includes 32 repetitions of *maharanna* (have mercy upon us)

1 The *seged* and *'astasrēyo* renditions of this Canticle draw more heavily upon the text in Daniel 3: 29-68. They also incorporate the acclamation *hālle* at the beginning of each verse: *hálle, hálle, yebārkewo* (all the stars of heaven bless ...).

The *semāʾe ʾesrāʾēl* is a bipartite prayer with a chanted introduction followed by a short responsorial setting incorporating the words *semāʾe ʾesrāʾēl* as a refrain. Although this prayer contains a portion of Deut. 6, it does not incorporate the entire *šema* text, nor does it recur in other Falasha rituals.[17]

The Music

(a) Pitch Content

The six Sabbath prayers share pentatonic melodic settings in two basic configurations.[18] (See Musical Example 1) The first configuration, "Category

Musical Example 1: Pitch Content of six *sanbat* prayers:

A", comprises a scale gapped at the third degree. *Negus ʾadonāy, ʾadonāy,* and *watebēlo sanbat* share this pitch content, although in *negus ʾadonāy*, the final stands in the middle of the range. *Waradat sanbat* resembles the other "Category A" prayers, but contains a lowered second scale degree. The two remaining prayers, *bārek sanbateye* and *semāʾe ʾesrāʾel*, contain pitch content gapped at the second scale degree; they are classified as "Category B".

---

17. See Kay K. Shelemay, "A Comparative Study: Jewish Liturgical Forms in the Falasha Liturgy?," *Yuval, Studies of the Jewish Music Research Centre*, (Jerusalem: forthcoming). The only similarities to normative Jewish Sabbath liturgy are the presence of brief sections from Psalm 146 in *ʾesēbho* and Psalm 150 within *ʾamlākeya*. There is no regular reading of Biblical portions in Falasha tradition.
18. Falasha musical examples contain both hemitonic and anhemitonic pentatonic forms, often incorporating more pitches than a "pure" five-tone system.

Other prayers within the Sabbath ritual share these configurations, most matching the pitch content of Category A. Several prayers share the lowered (or flexible) second scale degree with *waradat sanbat,* a structure which we can now confirm as a large sub-group within Category A. No statutory prayers fit fully within Category B, for the *kalḥu kwellu malā'ekt* also contains the second scale degree. Category B pitch content, however, is very common in other rituals, and both the *kalḥu kwellu malā'ekt* and *yetbārak* for evenings usually fall within this category on other occasions. The recitation of two prayers, *qeddus* and *genāyu,* is common to other morning rituals, although they are also frequently sung to Category A pitch content. (See Figure 4)

In addition to the extensive sharing of pitch content, both the Sabbath and statutory prayers share melodic contours. Most phrases are arch forms that end on a single repeated pitch. The frequent return to a central pitch, abundantly illustrated in the examples in Appendix 1, is characteristic of Ethiopian music. In Ethiopian secular music, the most important pitch of a tuning system or musical composition is termed the *malaš,* from *mallasa,* "to return". The *malaš* and its octave equivalents are sounded more often than other pitches and are always repeated in ending formulae.[19] Although the Falashas do not use the term *malaš* in discussion of sacred music, they do share the word for liturgical music, *zēmā,* with their Ethiopian Christian countrymen. In both traditions, *zēmā* incorporates all aspects of sacred music, including melody, rhythm, instrumental accompaniment, dance, and text. These factors, in addition to the firm grounding of Falasha melodies within a pentatonic system,[20] confirm the close relationship of Falasha music to those of other Ethiopian traditions.

(b) *Performance Practice*

Falashas also share antiphonal performance practice and related terminology with the Ethiopian Christian musical tradition. The Sabbath prayers presented here provide a relatively characteristic sample of performance styles. Most of the Falasha liturgy is performed in antiphonal style by two choruses of Falasha priests; the congregation, untrained in Geez, does not participate. When few priests are present, or during long rituals, two soloists, or a soloist and chorus will alternate. Most verses are sung twice, once by each choir or "side". All of these styles appear to be variations of the basic antiphonal arrangement.[21] (See Appendix 1, Examples B, D, and F)

19. Ashenafi Kebede, "The Bowl-Lyre of Northeast Africa. Krar: The Devil's Instrument," *Ethnomusicology* XXI. 3 (1977), 389-391.
20. B. Sarosi has written: "If we should have to characterize with one word musically those ... territories of Ethiopia... then that word would be: *pentatony.*" "The Music of the Ethiopian Peoples," *Studia Musicologica* IX, 1-2 (1967), 10.

Figure 4: Pitch Content of Prayers within *sanbat* Liturgy

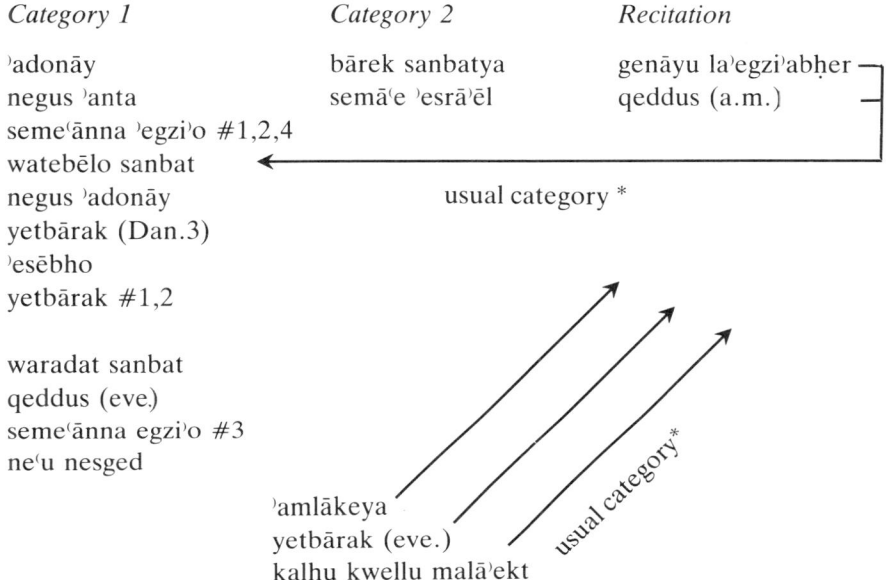

* Usual category signifies the usual melodic setting of indicated texts in other rituals.

In some portions of the liturgy, a word from the verse or the exclamation "Halleluya" is interpolated by the opposite chorus in the middle of a verse.[22] This second style may have its roots in responsorial form. (See Appendix 1, Examples A, C, and E)

Conclusions

Analysis of the six Sabbath prayers in their liturgical context enables us to conclude that 1) Sabbath prayers do not display musical settings distinct from

21. The use of two opposing choirs is an early Christian musical innovation unknown in the synagogue. Hanoch Avenary, "Formal Structure of Psalms and Canticles in Early Jewish and Christian Chant," *Musica Disciplina* 7 (1963), 1-13. Reprinted in *Encounters of East and West in Music* (Tel Aviv: Faculty of Visual and Performing Arts, Tel Aviv Univ., 1979), 111. Prof. Avenary has also commented in correspondence that the Falasha (and Ethiopian Christian) designation of double choirs as "sides" parallels Syrian Church practice. This may be particularly significant because of the documented impact of Syriac practice upon Ethiopian Christianity. See Ephraim Isaac, "An Obscure Component," 239-245.
22. Hanoch Avenary has also noted that the interpolation of "halleluya" within psalm verses is shared by Syriac practice. (Private correspondence)

others in the liturgy; and 2) morning and evening Sabbath prayers share musical content. Here we confront a discrepancy between informant exegesis and the available data. Although Falasha priests do not usually isolate what we classify as "musical data" from their textual-liturgical context, they indicate during interviews that their liturgical music changes both according to time of day and liturgical occasion. Yet the prayers examined here, and those previously studied from the *seged* pilgrimage,[23] show that all melodies used for these days can be found elsewhere in the Falasha liturgical cycle. Additionally, there do not seem to be clearcut distinctions in musical content for different times of day.

Comparative studies of Falasha and Ethiopian Christian liturgical music may provide answers to these issues. On-going analysis indicates that both specific melodies and modal structures are shared by Falasha and Ethiopian Christian liturgies. Ethiopian Christian *zēmā* divides into three categories of melody called *selt,* which are used alone or in close proximity on different liturgical occasions. If Falasha musical practice is similarly organized, then melodic usage can only be defined from the perspective of the entire liturgy. Therefore, occasions said to have distinctive musical identities, while sharing all their musical content with other rituals, may be explained by reference to a broader level of liturgical practice.[24]

We have seen that the Falasha Sabbath liturgy contains prayers evidently statutory to all Falasha rituals, indicating close relationships between different occasions in the Falasha liturgical cycle. The Falasha Sabbath also shares the prayers *yetbārak, ne'u nesged* and *'esēbḫo* with liturgies performed upon *seged* and *'astasrēyo.* The presence of the *yetbārak,* a Falasha version of the Apocryphal Canticle of the Three Youths in the Fire, is of particular interest since it is not found in Jewish liturgy. However, this prayer is an important element in contemporary Ethiopian Christian monastic liturgy.[25] The annual pilgrimage *seged* is a syncretic observance said to derive from Falasha monastic practice; it also shares both terminology and liturgical content with a contemporary Ethiopian Christian fast called *mehella.*[26] Therefore, we can

23. See Kay K. Shelemay, "Seged: A Falasha Pilgrimage Festival," *Musica Judaica* III, 1 (1980-1981), 43-62.
24. The problem is compounded by extensive use of contrafact within the liturgy. For example, the melody of a prayer used to open all annual holiday rituals (See Shelemay, "A Quarter-Century in the Life of a Falasha Prayer," *Yearbook of the International Folk Music Council* 19 (1978), 83-108) closely resembles that of the *bārek sanbateye* in pitch content and melodic contour. My attempts to clarify this issue during fieldwork with Falasha priests in Israel in summer, 1980, were unsuccessful.
25. Aymro Wondmagegnehu, *The Ethiopian Orthodox Church* (Addis Ababa: Ethiopian Orthodox Mission, 1970), 88. The complex relationship between this canticle and the statutory *yetbārak* will be explored in my book.
26. Shelemay, "Seged," 44.

trace a connection between the Falasha Sabbath liturgy and an occasion of probable Ethiopian Christian provenance.[27] Yet, we also find this same prayer shared by the Sabbath liturgy and that for *'astasrēyo*, a day of repentance linked by its significance and date of occurrence with the Jewish *Yom Kippur*. Therefore, Falasha occasions of both Judaic and monastic heritage share musical content, as well as liturgical texts.

The music and text of the Falasha Sabbath liturgy are but small portions of the Falasha liturgical cycle. Yet they are demonstrably representative of its textual and musical content, and of Ethiopian musical and liturgical traditions in general. Although the Falasha religion contains an amalgam of Jewish, Christian, and autochthonous elements, they are welded into an aesthetic whole in the musical/liturgical tradition. Clifford Geertz has written that cultural forms and their creators

> are brought into actual existence by the experience of living in the midst of certain sorts of things to look at, listen to, handle, think about, cope with, and react to... Art and the equipment to grasp it are made in the same shop.[28]

Our Sabbath sample indicates that the Falasha liturgy must have been unified, if not formulated, at a particular historical juncture by a single unifying force. Liturgical form and content provides evidence of a general sensibility shaped by a strict Sabbath observance, a Geez literary tradition, and musical expression typical of an Ethiopian milieu. A broad array of evidence – historical, linguistic, liturgical, and musical – suggests Falasha monks and their monastic sources in medieval Ethiopia as having provided the "shop" in which Falasha beliefs and their liturgical forms were shaped.[29] The music and text of the Sabbath liturgy therefore provides insight not only into Falasha liturgical/musical practice, but into the world view and sensibility that gave it both meaning and substance.

Acknowledgements

I would like to thank the following people for their help in researching and writing this article: Falasha priests of Ambober, Ethiopia, and Wubshet

27. The sharing of *yetbārak*, *ne'u nesged*, and *'esebḥo* within several morning rituals may also reflect portions of the Falasha Monastic Office. Although only the *yetbārak* is listed as part of the Office by my informants, Leslau's sources identified *ne'u nesged* as a prayer to be said at "forenoon." *Falasha Anthology*, 112. The occurrence of this prayer during the forenoon hours in *seged* and *'astasrēyo* rituals would support this hypothesis; however, their Sabbath morning appearance is before 7 a.m.
28. Geertz, "Art as a Cultural System," *Modern Language Notes* 19 (1976) 1473-1499.
29. Indeed, Falasha oral traditions credit a monk named Abba Sabra with formulating their liturgical cycle and composing their prayers. See Shelemay, "Historical Ethnomusicology," 237-238.

Atagab and Uri Ben Baruch of Israel, for exegesis concerning the Falasha liturgy and renditions of their prayers; Abba Petros Gebreselassie, for aiding in transcription and translation of the Sabbath prayer texts; Dr. Olga Kapeliuk, for suggesting corrections to the texts; and Prof. Hanoch Avenary, for his useful suggestions concerning the format and content of this article.

This article was written during a 1981-1982 fellowship year supported by the American Council of Learned Societies through a grant from the National Endowment for the Humanities.

Appendix 1: Transcriptions, Texts, and Translations

Key to Musical Transcriptions

'	slight pause
−	approximately a quarter-tone lower than written
+	approximately a quarter-tone higher than written
∿	trill
ᘯ	glottal stroke
c	chorus
s	solo

All musical examples are transcribed with final upon A to facilitate comparison and limit the use of accidentals. Examples are written in alto clef to minimize ledger lines; the music is usually sung in a high tenor range. The original pitch of the final for each example is indicated in parentheses at the beginning of each transcription.

Key to Textual Transcriptions
The foreign terms and texts, drawn from Amharic, Geez, and Hebrew, are transliterated according to the following system. Many consonants have approximately the same pronunciation as in English. The diacritical marks should be interpreted in the following way:
 č as in *ch*urch
 š as in *sh*oe
 ğ as in *j*oke
 ž as in plea*s*ure
 ň as in o*n*ion
 ṭ, c̣, p̣, q, and ṣ are glottalized or ejective sounds not found in English.

Geez and Amharic vowels are pronounced as follows:
i as in f*ee*t
ē as in st*a*te

ā as in *ah*
o as in n*o*r
u as in b*oo*t
a as in *uh* (sound made when hesitating while speaking)
e as in ros*e*s

Incomprehensible texts are indicated by ?.
Agau texts are indicated by ?A.
Syllables silent in speech are often pronounced when sung.

Musical Example A: *ʾadonāy*

1) ʾadonāy ṭeqa hēr ʾanta hāllēluyā ṭeqa hēr semekaʾamēn hāllēluyā
   Adonay, truly you are good, hallelujah, truly your name is good, amen, hallelujah
2) Agau
3) Agau
4) ʾadonāy manbaru baʾesāt kelul wamanṭalaʾetu zaberhānat qedam geṣe laleʿul ʾamēn hāllēluyā
   Adonay, his throne is surrounded by fire and a curtain of light is in front of his exalted face, amen, hallelujah

Text continues with intercession for sinners, parents, etc.
Total verses: 15

Musical Example B: *bārek sanbateya*

17

Bārek sanbateya "Bless my Sabbath"

1) bārek sanbatya ḥeyāwe yebē ʾegziʾabḥēr
   Bless my Sabbath, I am alive said the Lord
2) bārek sanbatyaʾeraftya waqedestya waburukteya wamāḥeyeweteya
   temaṣeʾe sanbata sanbat qadam badabra sinā badenq baʾesrāʾēl
   ḥeyāwe ʾana yebē ʾegziʾābḥēr
   Bless my Sabbath, holy and blessed, which gives me life.
   First Sabbath of Sabbaths comes from Mount Sinai, marvelous in Israel.
   I am alive, said the Lord.
3) bārek ʾakeberu sanbatātya wamalāʾekataya waʾakeberwāmu laqeddusānya
   wayeʾezēni kunu farāhē lafarāheyana ʾegziʾābḥēr ʾalbo zayegērem
   balāʿelēna??
   ḥeyāwe ʾana yebēʾegziʾābḥēr
   Bless and honor my Sabbath, and my angels, and honor my holy ones
   And now respect the one who is afraid of the Lord, there is nothing that
       frightens us ??
   I am alive, said the Lord.
4) bārek ʾana wahabkukemu sanbātat malāʾeket wamesala ʿeraftya
   waṣaweʾ u samya qeddus baʿelata sanbat
   yeʿeqab kwellomu ʾellataʾamanu watawakalu kiyāya sanbatya
   ḥeyāweʾana yebē ʾegziʾabḥēr
   Bless, I gave you Sabbaths, angels with my rest and call my holy name on
       the Sabbath day.
   Let those who trust and believe in me keep my Sabbath.
   I am alive, said the Lord.
5) bārek lasanbat sanbātya maʾekālēya wamāʾekalokemu waʾantemusa kama-
       za tekunu
   qeddusān ʿerufān neṣuḥān ʾesrāʾēl laʿālam
   ḥeyāwe ʾana yebē ʾegziʾabḥēr
   Bless the Sabbath, my Sabbath will be between you and me and you will
       be like that.
   Holy, peaceful, clean Israel forever.
   I am alive, said the Lord.

Text continues with description of giving of Law to Moses at Mt. Sinai, and warnings to observe the Sabbath.
Verse total: 13

Musical Example C: *waradat sanbat*

Waradat sanbat "The Sabbath descended"

1) waradat sanbat em'areyām
   Sabbath descended from the highest heaven.
2) waradat sanbat 'emdiba 'areyām
   Sabbath descended from above the highest heaven.
3) waradat sambat la'iyerusālēm
   Sabbath descended to Jerusalem.

Text continues with description of Sabbath's descent to earth.
Includes verses in Agau at end.
Verse total: 25

Musical Example D: *watebēlo sanbat*

watebēlo sanbat "And the Sabbath said"

1) watebēlo sanbat la'egzi'o sanbat 'eraft waqeddest waburekt
       wamāheyāwit la'egzi'abḥēr
   habani lita 'emkwello bafaqāda 'ageberta zi'aya
   And Sabbath said to the Lord, the Sabbath is rest and holy and blessed
       and gives life to the Lord.
   Give to me from all by the will of my servant.

2) ʾegziʾe ʾegziʾeya ʾahazē kwello ʿālam
   Lord, my Lord, holder of the whole world.
3) ʾegziʾe ʾegziʾeya faṭarē kwello feṭerata ʿālam
   Lord, my Lord, holder of the whole world.
3) ʾegziʾe ʾegziʾeya faṭarē kwello feṭerata ʿālam
   Lord, my Lord, creator of all the creatures of the world.
4) ʾegziʾe ʾegziʾeya fawāsē kwello laḥemumān*
   Lord, my Lord, healer of all the sick.
5) ʾegziʾe ʾegziʾeya balāḫē kwello lamendebān*
   Lord, my Lord, deliverer of all those who are trapped.

Text continues with Sabbath interceding on behalf of sinners.
Verse total: 12

* The correct constructions in these lines would be kwellomu ḥemumān, kwellomu mendebān, etc.

Musical Example E: *negus ʾadonāy*

Negus ʾadonāy "King, Adonay"

Negus ʾadonāy taʾamer kona ʾaḥādu ʾegziʾena
ʾegziʾe ʾadonāy lakwellu meder
ʾadonāy ʾaḥadu weʾetuʾ adonāy ʾamlākana
ʾadonāy aḥadu semu labāḫetitu
ʾadonāy semu lamangestu
ʾaḥadu ʾadonāy ʾamlākena
ʾadonāy negusena
ʾadonāy feṭārina
ʾadonāy gabārina
ʾadonāy aqābina
ʾadonāy nolāwina
ʾadonāy malākina
ʾadonāy watesfāna

King Adonay, a miracle will be, our Lord is one
Adonay is Lord to all the earth
Adonay is one, he is Adonay our God
Adonay his name is the only one
His name is one to his kingdom
One, Adonay, is our God
Adonay our king
Adonay our creator
Adonay our maker
Adonay our guardian
Adonay our shepherd
Adonay our ruler
Adonay our hope.
(Complete)

Musical Example F: *wayebē semā'e'esrā'ēl*

* ? ? ? : The incomprehensible passage in this example is 32 beats in length, ♩ =138.

Wayebē semā'e 'esrā'ēl (And he said, Hear Israel)

wayebē semā'e 'esrā'ēl 'egzi'abḫēr ??? (incomprehensible for 32 beats, ♩ = 138)
And he said, Hear Israel, the Lord ??

wa'afqero la'egzi'abḫēr 'amlākeka bakwellu lebeka wabakwellu nafsaka wabakwellu ḫayleka
And love the Lord your God with all your heart, and with all your soul, and with all your might

wayemlā'e westa lebeka
And let it fill your heart.

Divergency of Theory and Practice in Japanese Buddhist Chant

János Kárpáti, *Budapest*

Buddhism reached the Japanese islands, in the 6th century A.D., by way of China and Korea. Each of its numerous sects considers chant, together with a particular kind of instrumental music, to be an important element of liturgical practice. Among these sects, however, there are two which emerge with their strictly-preserved traditions as the true centers of Buddhist chant of Indian origin, the so-called *shōmyō*. One, the Tendai sect, was founded by Dengyō Daishi in 784 near Kyōtō in the Hiei-Zan mountain monastery, considered since that time to be the center of the Tendai school. The other, located in the Koya-San mountain monastery, is the center of the Shingon sect, founded in 816.

The traditions of *shōmyō* have been discussed in a fairly rich literature from the 9th century onward. This literature contains historical notes on the life and activities of the great masters as well as theoretical texts and – to a lesser extent – notations of melodies. The first important scholar in the history of *shōmyō* notation was Riōnin, from the Tendai school. He worked out a relatively developed notation system in the first decades of the 12th century, but without indicating the exact pitch: thus his method essentially follows the principle of *neuma*.

Also the masters belonging to the Shingon sect played an important part in developing further the theory and practice of the *shōmyō*, it was Kakui, the monk, who in the 13th century introduced the method of *goin-hakase*, a notation using five pitches. Not unlike Guido d'Arezzo in Europe, he led the musical practice to greater accuracy, abolishing the earlier habit of merely relying on the memory in Buddhist liturgical chant.

It was also in the 13th century that the first great theoretical compendium of the *shōmyō* was completed by Tanchi (1163–1240) from the Tendai school. Under the title *Shōmyō Yōjinshū*, the voluminous scroll-manuscript dating from 1233 became the "Ars Nova" of the Buddhist world, because it was fiercely opposed by the more conservative representatives of the liturgy. Two and a half centuries later the theoretical basis provided by the *Shōmyō Yōjinshū* was further developed by Chōe, a follower of the Shingan school. His work, *Gyosan Taigaischu*, written in 1498,[1] is the greatest textbook of Buddhist liturgy, still definitive even today.

---

1. The manuscript, consisting of two scrolls, has undergone many revisions and woodprint reproductions in the course of the centuries. The last revised edition was issued by the Koyasan University in 1925. Eta Harich-Schneider, *A History of Japanese Music*, (London, 1973), p. 324.

In this voluminous text, the full theoretical system of the *shōmyō* is considered in detail on the basis of a minute description and a synopsis of its melodic structures as well as its rhythmic and metrical patterns. The theoretical literature of the following centuries did not add much to this knowledge; at most it elaborated some of its details. According to the historical sources, the art of *shōmyō* undoubtedly declined during the 17th and 18th centuries, probably under the influence of political and social factors. Only in the 19th century, a conscious revival movement was started with the aim of recovering and systematizing the practice of *shōmyō* which had acquired numerous variations due to the existence of the different Buddhist sects.

At the present time, we see again a renaissance of the *shōmyō*, especially as a result of up-to-date scientific methods applied to it in Japan. Although a disappointing falsification of the liturgical traditions has been experienced (the use of the harmonium, for example), nevertheless, excellent recordings have been made, as well as scientific essays published. These activities demonstrate optimistic endeavors towards preservation of the *shōmyō*.[2]

The more recent essays – according to the best of my knowledge – have not yet appropriately confronted the great theoretical literature of the Middle Ages with current practice. Only the article written by Prof. Kataoka in *MGG* provides us with a short reference to the fact that, due to the decay of the *shōmyō* during the 17th and 18th centuries, a gap did develop between the theory (including the textbooks) and the practice of actual chant.[3] The European musician, however, being unaware of some deeper connections, will perceive more distinctly the divergence of theory and practice.

According to the two great theoretical works of the 13th and 15th century, the cardinal point of the theory of *shōmyō* are two anhemitonic pentatonic scales taken over from Chinese tradition in their original form. These are as follows:

(a) the *ryō* scale with the structure $D - E - F\ sharp - A - B$; and

(b) the *ritsu* scale with $D - E - G - A - B$.

---

2.   Eta Harich-Schneider, "Le chant bouddhique japonais: le shô-myo" in: *Encyclopédie des musiques sacrées*, ed. Jacques Porte, Vol. I, pp. 199–213. Gido Kataoka, "La musique de la liturgie bouddhique au Japon" in: *Centre d'Etudes de Musique Orientale*, Bulletin No. 2, Paris, 1968.
Records: "Buddhist Music": *The Music of Japan* Vol. IV in: *A Musical Anthology of the Orient* – UNESCO Collection. Bärenreiter-Musicaphon BM 30 L 2015. *Shōmyō Tendai*. Polydor MN 9001–1/4. *Shōmyō Shingon*. Polydor MN 9001–1/4. *Tendai-shū daigernryū shōmyō daizen*. King Record KGT 1–12.
3.   *Die Musik in Geschichte und Gegenwart*... Hrsg. von F. Blume. Bd. 12, Spalte 643–649.

Japanese theory, however, strove to introduce not only these two scales but, together with them, also the principle of the twelve possible transpositions offered by the Chinese *lü*. This system is so highly sophisticated that it is nearly impossible to use it in the vocal practice of the liturgical repertoire.

The further development of the theory of *shōmyō* seems to eliminate this contradiction by limiting the modal circle to only five modes out of the twelve possible transpositions by keeping the scales based on $D - E - G - A - B$ with the structure of either the *ryō*, or the *ritsu* scales.

The existence and vitality of anhemitonic pentatonics can be studied relatively easily in the syllabic and reciting layer of the repertoire, called *tendoku*. In some of the chants of the repertoire even the formation of the pentatonic set of tones may be traced without presupposing any kind of chronology or method of planning. Let us first examine a recitative making use of only three tones: Example 1

In this example, the permanent cadence pattern of the *F–G–D* structure can be perceived very well at the end of the particular lines or units, respectively. This example is of special interest because the singer transposes the *tonus currens*[4] and the cadence connected with it to various levels, making use somehow of the possibility of "modulation" or, *métabole*,[5] the term chosen by Brailoiu. Such change of mode is known as *hennon* in the theory of *shōmyō*, but it is with some uncertainty that the literature reports its existence or occurrence in recent times. Example 2

---

4. Because of certain analogies with the plainsong tradition we use the terminology of the European Gregorian Chant.
5. Constantin Brăiloiu, *Problèmes d'ethnomusicologie*, G. Rouget, Genève, 1973.

Example 2 shows that the figurations may sometimes move upward from the rather constant pitch *F* as far as *A*. Therefore, it is not suprising that the three-tone seed of pentatonics will grow into a four-tone form of the following structure: *C sharp – E – F sharp – A*. From here it is only one step to reach the complete set of five tones in the mode structured *B – C sharp – E – F sharp – G sharp – B*. As an example of this process, the hymn-like chant called *Dai-San*, one of the most important items of the *shōmyō* repertoire, is quoted: Example 3

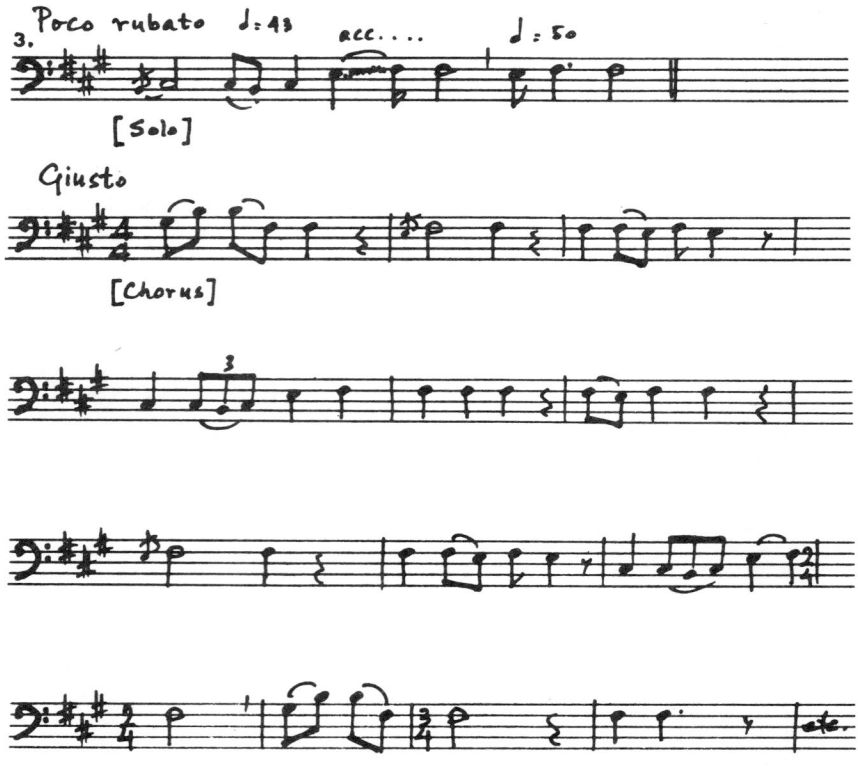

The examples given here are taken from the repertoire of the Tendai School since it was possible to study this material more closely. Based on these we may perhaps conclude that the above example may in fact be considered the *only* case to show the practical realization of the theoretically discussed pentatonic as a clear and unambigous manifestation of the anhemitonic five-tone *ritsu* (*D – E – G – A – B*).

The question arises, however, why there are no examples to show the scale of the *ryo* type. The Tendai collections of Polydor (4 records) and King Record (12 cassettes) support our statement that no case is found to show the unambigous occurrence of any music based, even partly, on the *ryo* scale, as happened with the above example of *ritsu*. It is, though, a striking fact that tunes having a scale structure of *D – F – G – B flat* are found relatively abundantly.

The types shown in the above examples have mainly a syllabic, reciting – or, as we may call it, "psalmodic" – character. An important part of the *shōmyō* repertoire, however, – almost its overwhelming majority – consists of richly-figured tunes of a melismatic character.[6]

The melismatic style of the *shōmyō* is governed by a peculiar principle: structures are formed by connecting melodic elements, characteristic variations and patterns consisting of two, three or more tones. These elements of melody and patterns have been preserved by the traditions of the two great schools.

In fact, after examining about twenty various melodic elements from the material of the Tendai School, it can be said that most of them consist of three or four tones and have the following structure: *D – F – G* and/or *D – F – G – B flat*, respectively. Here are some examples supporting this statement:
Example 4

It must be stated, nevertheless, that some degrees in these patterns oscillate, and that the anhemitonic structure will frequently be substituted by a hemitonic one. The most characteristic change is that of the structure *D – F – G – B flat* into *D – F sharp – G – B flat*.

6.   We cannot go into details of distinguishing between the syllabic-recitative and the embellished-melismatic styles of *shōmyō*. It must be said, however, that in the reading of sūtras the syllabic recitation and in the hymn-like chants (*e.g.*, *san* and *bai*) melismatic singing predominates.

A semitone may appear either above or below the major third and, in this way, the characteristic Japanese *hemitonic* pentatonics emerge – if not in full scale, then at least in part. This is rather important because, in the repertoire of *shōmyō*, the richly figured melismatic style (historically connected with the most ancient layer) shows the anhemitonic pentatonics of the Chinese type at most in traces, as in the following: Example 5

All this directs attention to the fact that the theoretical system of the great medieval textbooks, concerning the anhemitonic basic scales of the Chinese type, is only a fiction; in reality, it is *an artifical transplantation of the theory of the gagaku* – the court music considered in those times as the art of the highest level. The vocal tradition of the *shōmyō*, belonging to the religious practice of Buddhism, was more or less resistant to this influence and developed its characteristic Japanese style, more suitable to actual conditions of the society. The practice of *shōmyō* was also modified accordingly,[7] due to the fact that in Japanese folk music hemitonic pentatonics play a leading role.

Meanwhile, all that has been discussed here rests only on an hypothetical basis. A more exact answer, closer to the final one, can be outlined only after having studied the style of the other schools and, principally, with further support provided by our Japanese colleagues.

---

7. Even an opposite example can prove how decisive a factor the environment is: in the Chinese Buddhist liturgy the *anhemitonic* pentatony survives unchanged, as a manifestation of the instinctive musical feeling of the people. (*Cf.* with recorded Buddhist music from Taiwan, Lyrichord LLST 7222.)

Toward Comparative Study of Persian Radifs: Focus on Dastgāh-E Māhour

Bruno Nettl and Daryoosh Shenassa,[1] *Urbana-Champaign*

Four Radifs

The literature dealing with the radif of Persian classical music, by now extensive, emphasizes a consensus to the effect that a single body of material, comprised of twelve dastgāhs (or modes), each consisting of a number of subdivisions (gushehs), has for at least a century existed in a number of related variant forms. Attempts to publish in Western notation some of these versions, those regarded as particularly authoritative, have probably resulted in a decrease in the amount of variation, to which the concentration of musical life in Tehran in the period after 1940 has contributed. The publication, in 1963, of the radif of Musa Ma'roufi and its subsequent adoption as a standard by many musicians and some institutions seems to have caused some decline in the number of variants of the radif (or, put more simply, of radifs) extant and used.[2] But there is ample evidence[3] that the early twentieth century saw considerable diversity. The existence of a number of radifs is mentioned in much of the literature, with emphasis in some cases on the unity of the radif concept and with the belief that what is at hand is a single work with variants, in other cases on the development, by each master, on his own radif. Comparisons of radifs of different teachers have not been made in detail, and where extant, have sometimes been used for the purpose of providing archetypal versions[4] and to exhibit differences in size and total content.[5] Moreover, comparisons made so far have taken into account the radifs mentioned in the literature of the early twentieth century and known largely from names of their sections but not from their specific melodic content. Regarding these early radifs, more is known about the presence or absence of the names of particular dastgāhs or gushehs than about the commonality of musical material.

1. This paper is part of a larger study of the radifs of Persian music being carried out by the authors. For the materials in this paper, Shenassa worked as Nettl's research assistant during 1980–81 under a grant from the University of Illinois Research Board, whose support is gratefully acknowledged.
2. E. Zonis, *Classical Persian Music, an Introduction* (Cambridge, Mass., 1973), p. 65.
3. Kh. Khatschi, *Der Dastgāh* (Regensburg, 1962), *passim;* M.T. Massoudieh, *Āwāz-e Šur* (Regensburg, 1968), p. 19.
   E. Gerson-Kiwi, *The Persian Doctrine of Dastga-Composition; a phenomenological study in the musical modes*. Tel-Aviv (Israel Music Institute), 1963.
4. H. Farhat, *The Dastgāh Concept in Persian Music* (Los Angeles, UCLA, dissertation, 1965).
5. Khatschi, *op. cit.*

Our purpose in this paper is to move towards a comparative study of the radifs used in recent decades, and to do this, where possible, on the basis of recorded rather than notated versions. Although even in the 1970's a considerable number of musicians with their personal radifs appear to have been active, there are a few radifs that have clearly been dominant in Tehran. Among them are those of Ma'roufi,[6] already noted above, which was published with the blessing of the Ministry of Fine Arts, and therefore used as a reference source by academic musicians; of Abolhassan Sabā,[7] leading figure in the development of the Conservatory of National Music (Honārestān-e Musiqi-ye Melli), whose radif is published in a set of widely used instruction books; Nour-Ali Boroumand, a distinguished musician and teacher whose radif became official in the development of the Iranian music section of the University of Tehran Music Department in the late 1960's;[8] and Mahmoud Karimi, the leading teacher of the vocal radif, whose material, in transcription and recording, was eventually published by the Ministry of Fine Arts as a vocal counterpart to Ma'roufi's instrumental radif.[9]

In this paper, we make a variety of observations based on comparative study of the dastgāh of Māhour as it is found in these four radifs. All but that of Sabā are available to us in recorded form, and all but that of Boroumand are also published in Western notation. We should point out, however, the different purposes of the notations. Karimi's radif was recorded as sung by himself, and the recordings transcribed by a trained ethnomusicologist, Mohammad T. Massoudieh. Ma'roufi's was published in a transcription made by the author, who was also a performer; the recorded version available to us was made by Soleiman Ruh-Afzā who evidently used the printed music. Sabā's notations, on the other hand, are not transcriptions of performance, as far as one can tell, but were made by the author from his memory. The Ma'roufi and Sabā notations are technically prescriptive, made

6. M. Barkechli, *La musique traditionelle de l'Iran: Les Systèmes de la musique traditionelle de l'Iran (Radif), avec transcription en notation musicale occidentale par Moussa Ma'roufi* (Tehran, 1963).
7. The first publication dates of Saba's instruction books are obscure, but go back to the 1940's. Editions available to us date from the 1950's and 1960's, but appear to be essentially reprints. The books appear with analogous titles, e.g., *Doreh-ye Avval-e Violon* (first course for violin), or *Doreh-ye Sevvom-e Santour* (third course for santour), etc. The layout for the four books in the santour radif may be of interest: 1st course Segāh and Shur; 2nd course Bayāt-e Tork, Abū-Atā, Afshāri, and Dashti (the four dastgāhs derivative of Shur); 3rd course: Homayoun, Bayāt-e Esfahān, and Chahārgāh; 4th course: Māhour, Navā, and Rāst-Panjgāh.
8. B. Nettl, "Nour-Ali Boroumand, a Twentieth-Century Master of Persian Music," *Studia Instrumentorum Musicae Popularis* 3 (1975), pp. 167–71.
9. M. Karimi, *Radif vocal de la musique traditionelle de l'Iran. Transcription et analyse par Mohammad Taghi Massoudieh* (Tehran, 1978).

for practical instruction of Iranian students, although Ma'roufi may also have a substantial descriptive component. That of Karimi is descriptive, made for purposes of ethnomusicological analysis.

In most respects, we have in our work used the recordings. It is important to bear in mind the fact that these four radifs come from a variety of orders of source material. Even so, we may feel justified in using them for comparative study, as all four are available to us in the forms in which they were transmitted to the Iranian musicians who studied them and used them as basis of improvisation and performance. We also remind the reader that what we are comparing is not performances of Persian music itself, but performed versions of what is taught to students so that they in turn will have a basis for performing true music.

The four radifs came into existence in a variety of ways. That of Ma'roufi began as the creation of a committee appointed to standardize the radif into an official version but, since committee creations may be difficult to realize, resulted finally from the work of the leading member of this committee who, we suspect, developed the details of organization in the course of doing the work.[10] We do not know to what extent Ma'roufi used different forms of the radif in his work as a teacher from year to year, or to what degree the published version reflects his personal version in study and teaching. His radif is the longest, having the greatest number of gushehs and the longest versions of these. Boroumand's radif is the most similar to Ma'roufi's, and since Boroumand once studied with him, there is some reason to suspect that Ma'roufi's publication does indeed reflect his personal practice. The version of Boroumand's radif used by us comes from recordings made about 1975. However, recordings of portions of his radif as performed by him were also made in 1966, 1968, and 1969 (by B. Nettl and Stephen Blum, and by Boroumand himself), and on the whole these agree with the 1975 recording. Disagreements as often concern names given to melodic sections as they do the identity of the melodic materials. In any event, Boroumand's radif was evidently thoroughly worked out from a number of sources by the 1930's or 1940's, and learned aurally (as Boroumand was blind). And the form in which it is used here was that which Boroumand taught in the 1970's, as observed by the authors in Tehran.

Karimi's radif was evidently also recorded in a form which he used in teaching. It is possible to compare the version recorded by him for the published form in the 1970's with performances made by him for field recordings by Nettl in 1968–69, and by Tsuge[11] in the late 1960's. Here the

10. Zonis, *op. cit.*, p. 63.
11. G. Tsuge, *Āvāz: a Study of the Rhythmic Aspects in Classical Persian Music* (Middletown, Conn., Wesleyan University, dissertation, 1974.)

agreement among versions performed several years apart is greater even than in Boroumand's case. Sabā's radif comes in a different form again. He published a number of instruction books for individual instruments – two sets for violin, one for santour, and one for tār or setār. Each set contains two to four volumes, and these books are labeled as his "radif" and organized by dastgāhs. But within the context of one dastgāh may be found gushehs properly part of a radif and also Sabā's own compositions, and in no one book is there an attempt to present the entire radif. What we have available for this study, therefore, is a composite of all of Sabā's instruction books, although the set for santour, being the most elaborate and including representative sections of all twelve dastgāhs, has been most used. Certainly the kind of material from which the Sabā radif derives differs not only in substance and style but also in fundamental genesis from the other radifs which, indeed, differ considerably from each other in some of these respects as well.

A comprehensive comparison of the four radifs, for which this is a pilot study, would result in a book-length manuscript requiring painstaking examination of a vast number of short melodic sections in their content and designation as well as their position. We present a sample of such a comparison. We are interested in a comparison of its overall organization, and of detailed comparison of individual sections taking into account their identity in terms of name as well as of melodic content. We wish to know how different musicians have labeled the same music, and about the representation of one or a number of different melodic segments by one name. We are also interested in internal interrelationships within a radif, that is, in the kinds of relationships found within a dastgāh, and among the dastgāhs of one radif; and the degree to which similar interrelationships of this sort are found among the four radifs examined.

Comparison of Designations

Proceeding to the comparison of the Māhour sections, we turn first to consideration of the number of gushehs used in each radif, and to their names. It is necessary to keep in mind that the melodic content of gushehs of the same name may differ, while gushehs with similar musical content may be present in different radifs under a variety of names. Table I gives the names of the gushehs found in the four radifs. The number of gushehs clearly varies; but this is in part due to the lack of standardization in nomenclature. Yet some gushehs are simply absent in certain radifs; Khosravāni, for example, is found in Ma'roufi and Boroumand, in the tār or setār books of Sabā (but not in his others), but is absent in Karimi.

The names of the gushehs themselves present an interesting study; they come from various sources and fall into several categories. Some are place-names (*e.g.*, Arāq, "Iraq") or personal names (Abol). More common are adjectival forms indicating places (Āzarbāyjāni), or place names to which diminutive particles have been added (Neshaburak, referring to Nishapour, or Esfahānak – which may refer not to the city but to the dastgāh, Bayat-e Isfahan). Adjectival forms of personal names appear such as Hajji Hassani and Khosravāni (referring to Khosrow). Common nouns which may refer to sounds or to texts no longer used, such as Zangouleh ("little bell") are found, as are adjectives that may have affective significance (Skekasteh – "broken"; and Delkash – "fascinating"). Some names, such as Chahār pareh (four-parts) indicate formal features. Some gushehs bear the name of a musical function in a dastgāh, as Darāmad, "coming-in" or introduction, which begins each dastgāh, or Moqadameh ("preface"). A few, such as Feili, seem to be words with no meaning other than the designation of a gusheh.

Variation of nomenclature for essentially the same material is particularly conspicuous in the presentation of the introductory gushehs which are central to the concept of a dastgāh. Māhour in each radif has material that one might designate as the Darāmad group, and in each case there are at least three characteristic units of musical content:

a) a motif which moves from a tonic to the fourth below;
b) a section with the characteristic kereshmeh rhythm, ♪♩ ♪♩ ♩ ♫♩♩ or a variant thereof, beginning with the fifth degree and moving gradually up to the tonic; and
c) a section beginning on the fourth degree and moving down to the tonic.

All four "darāmad" groups therefore contain essentially the same material, but the order and designation of subdivisions varies. Thus, Ma'roufi begins with Moqadameh (which contains the material above designated as "a"), moves to a metric gusheh designated as Koroghli, then to Kereshmeh (containing "b"), to First Darāmad (recapitulating Moqadameh, or "a"), Second Darāmad ("c"), and Āvāz (continuation of "c"). Boroumand divides the darāmad group into three sections: First Darāmad ("a"), Kereshmeh ("b"), and Āvāz ("c"). Sabā, in his radif for tār or setār, has two sections, labeled Darāmad-e Benafsheh, containing "a" and "b", and Darāmad-e Qadim ("c"). Karimi presents the entire darāmad group in one section, labeled simply Darāmad, and containing, briefly, a, b, a, and c. The term Moqadameh is used sometimes to introduce the darāmad group, but may also identify an introductory section to another gusheh, as in the case of Boroumand's Moqadameh-ye Dād, preceding the gusheh Dād. In some cases, Moqadameh implies material later also given in the main gusheh; in

Table I. The Gushehs of Māhour, by Name, and their Distribution in the Four Radifs.

	Ma'roufi	Boroumand	Karimi	Sabā
Moqaddameh	X			
Kereshmeh	X	X		X
Darāmad	X	X	X	X
Goshāyesh	X		X	X
Dād	X	X	X	X
Khosravāni	X	X		X
Delkash	X	X	X	X
Hāj Hassani	X			
Khārazmi or	X		X	
Majles Afruz				(X)
Khāvarān	X	X	X	X
Tarab Angiz	X	X		X
Neishāburak	X	X	X	
Tusi and/or	X	X	X	X
Nasir Khāni	X	(X)	X	
Chāhār Pāreh and/or	X	X		
Morād Khāni		(X)	X	
Āzarbāyjāni	X	X	X	X
Feili	X	X	X	X
Zir Afkand	X	X	X	X
Mahur-E Saqir	X	X	X	X
Hesār-E Māhur	X	X		
(Hesār) and/or				
Abol	X	(X)	X	X
(Āvāz-E Abol)	X			
Neiriz	X	X		X
(Gusheh-E Neiriz)			X	
Skekasteh	X	X	X	X
Nahib	X	X	X	X
Sorush	X			
Arāq	X	X	X	X
Mohayyer	X	X		X
Āshur or	X		X	
Āshur Āvand		X		X
Basteh Negār	X			X
Esfahānak	X	X		X
Hazin	X	X	X	X
Rāk and/or	X			X
Member(s) of Rāk family	X	X	X	X
Masnavi	X		X	X
Mirzāib				X
Sāqi Nāmeh	X	X	X	X

others, such as Moqadameh be Greyli in the dastgāh of Shur, it is clearly distinct and separate. The term Āvāz, while on the one hand referring to the entire non-metric portion of a classical performance, is used in the radif to indicate a variety of materials. In Ma'roufi, it normally follows a gusheh designated by a distinctive name. Elsewhere it may substitute for Darāmad, as in the Māhour section of Sabā's radifs for violin.

But while introductory gushehs in the dastgāh of Māhour have the greatest amount of terminological variation, variety is also found further on. For example, a melodic entity is identified by Boroumand at different points as Chahār Pareh and Morad Khāni, while these two names represent two different melodic entities in the radifs of Karimi and Ma'roufi. Variants of a gusheh appearing in one radif may also be designated in such a way as to show relationships, as in the case of Rāk-e Hendi, Rāk-e Keshmir, and Rāk-e Abdollah in Boroumand's radif, where they are clearly variations of the same melodic material. The term "gusheh" itself may precede the name of a particular gusheh. The name, "gusheh Neiriz" in Karimi's Māhour is called simply "Neiriz" by Ma'roufi and Boroumand.

What is to be noted in the comparison of radifs is the fact that there is more difference in nomenclature than in musical content. Differences in the latter involve occasional omission of materials elsewhere present rather than outright contradiction.

The "Common" Gushehs

Viewing Māhour in the four radifs again in terms of designation of materials, there are twenty gushehs which are found in all. Since Iranian music masters place considerable emphasis on the order in which the materials appear in a dastgāh, it is interesting to compare the orders (see Table II). The composite nature of the radif of Sabā presents a special problem. His radif for santour includes most of the twenty "common" gushehs of Māhour, lacking only Dād, Neyriz, Nahib, and Rāk-e Abdollāh. Based on the position which each of these occupies in the other Sabā radifs, we have suggested a place for each of these four gushehs in a santour radif; thus the order given here for Sabā is that of santour radif, with the four lacking gushehs in those places in which we believe he would have presented them.

What strikes one first is the considerable degree of agreement among the orders of these common gushehs in the four radifs. Particularly to be noted is the identical order at the beginning and end of the listing. The first two common gushehs, Darāmad (*i.e.*, the entire Darāmad group as discussed above) and Dād appear in this order. The last eight of the twenty also appear

Table II. The Twenty Common Gushehs of Māhour, and their Order. The Basic Order is that of Boroumand; the columns at the right indicate the order of these gushehs in the other three Radifs.

NO.		Ma'roufi	Karimi	Sabā
1	Darāmad	1	1	1
2	Dād	2	2	(2)
3	Delkash	3	9	8
4	Khāvarān	4	10	5
5	Tusi	5	7	6
6	Feili	8	8	10
7	Māhur-E Saqir	6	6	9
8	Āzarbāyjāni	10	12	7
9	Hesār-E Māhur	7	3	12
10	Zir Afkand	9	11	(11)
11	Neiriz	11	5	3
12	Shekasteh	12	4	4
13	Arāq	14	14	(14)
14	Nahib	13	13	13
15	Mohayyer	15	15	15
16	Āshur Āvand	16	16	16
17	Hazin	17	17	17
18	Rāk-E Abdollāh	19	19	19
19	Safir-E Rāk	18	18	(18)
20	Sāqi Nāmeh	20	20	20

in the same order: Nahib, Arāq, Mohayyer, Ashour Avand, Hazin, Safir-e Rāk, Rāk-e Abdollāh, and Saqināmeh, in the radifs of Ma'roufi, Karimi, and Sabā, and in only a slightly different order in Boroumand, where two pairs of gushehs, Arāq and Nahib, and Rāk-e Abdollāh and Safir-e Rāk, are reversed.

There is less agreement in the order of appearance of the remaining ten of the common gushehs: Delkash, Khāvarān, Tousi, Āzarbāyjāni, Feili, Zir-Afkan, Māhour-Saqir, Hasār-e Māhour, Neyriz, and Shekasteh. Yet their order also indicates a fundamental patterning. Thus, Delkash is immediately followed by Khāvarāh in three radifs, as the third and fourth gushehs in Ma'roufi and Boroumand, and as ninth and tenth Karimi. Neyriz and Shekasteh are adjacent in all four radifs. Feili usually appears after Delkash; the two are about equidistant in three of the radifs, but adjacent, in reverse order in Karimi's.

It is worth noting that in the corpus we have examined, no two gushehs, and no two versions of any gusheh, are absolutely identical. There are a few instances in which similarity is very great, as in Khāvarān in the Boroumand and Ma'roufi radifs. More frequently, however, great similarity is found in the melodic content at the opening and therefore characteristic sections of like-named gushehs, after which there is greater divergence. The differences at this point result from extension or elimination of melodic figures, rather than from the presence of unrelated materials. Occasionally, however, versions of a gusheh in different radifs exhibit similarity in the middle section rather than the beginning; for example, Rāk-e Abdollāh in Boroumand and Sabā's radif for tār or setār.

Finally, a few gushehs with the same name share no melodic content and would appear to be different entities which have somehow been given the same name. An example is Moradkhāni in the radifs of Boroumand and Karimi, where there is no resemblance. Instead, Boroumand's Moradkhāni is similar to Karimi's Nasirkhāni. But such examples are rare.

Normally, then, melodic content and names coincide. But if reckoned by content rather than name, the "common" gushehs appear in slightly different order than that indicated by our list of gushehs by name.

Rhythmic Considerations

While it has been generally assumed that the major differences among radifs and among the sections of a radif can be perceived best through the use of melodic and modal criteria, it should not be taken for granted that rhythmic elements may not also play a role. The earlier literature does not deal with rhythm very much. In most cases, the bifurcation of Persian music in two types, composed and improvised, is continued in a dichotomy between metric and non-metric. Tsuge deals with rhythmic aspects of the vocal radif, but does so mainly by associating them with metric analysis of Persian poetry.[12] Farhat[13] discusses various types of material within the radif as having a greater or lesser degree of metric regularity, but does not go into great detail on what this means. His classification of the content of radifs as consisting of gushehs and tekkes, the former typically non-metric and prone to far-flung variation in improvisation, the latter more typically performed the same way every time and likely to have rhythmic regularity, is insightful. Persian musicians, in dealing with the issue in a practical way, move further in the same direction. Their terminology includes a number of kinds of music which are distinguished chiefly or importantly by their rhythmic character. Āvāz implies generally non-metric structure. Zarbi implies metric structure in general. Chahār mezrāb adds to it a rhythmic ostinato. Naghmeh, at least according to Boroumand, implies a non-metric performance with considerable prevalence of one note value. Kereshmeh and Chahār pareh imply specific rhythmic patterns in an irregular metric scheme often performed rubato and broken by non-metric bits.

The impression one receives on hearing a large section of a radif, such as an entire dastgāh, is that it is essentially non-metric, and readily distinguished from consistently metric composed pieces such as pishdarāmad or tasnif. But it is also clear that rhythmic movement of many kinds follow each other in quick succession. One way of using the Persian musician's tendency to develop musical classes on the basis of rhythmic criteria is to identify a number of kinds of rhythmic movement that one may find in the radif, and to plot their distribution. In order to investigate this approach further, we established an informal typology of rhythm in categories based on several overlapping criteria, including the degree of dominance by one note value, the presence or absence of a regular succession of beats, repetiton of short or long rhythmic motifs, and consistency of tempo. The following list is not presented as a typology but rather as an illustration of a way in which the large variety of kinds of rhythmic movement might be grouped and described.

A – completely non-metric movement with no perceptible regularity of any sort.
B – a slow section with a few tones of roughly the same length.
C – a faster section with a few tones of roughly the same length.

12. Tsuge, *op. cit.* See also his "Rhythmic Aspects of Āvāz in Persian Music," *Ethnomusicology* 14 (1970), pp. 205–27.
13. Farhat, *op. cit.*, pp. 243–44.

D – a rhythmic pattern which is repeated but is internally non-metric, something frequently found in connection with melodic sequence.

E – a relatively long section in which most notes are in one standard note length or its value doubled, *e.g.*, quarter and eighth notes. Some sections designated "naghmeh" begin with it.

F – short metric bits, with a beat clearly present, separated by pauses, presented in rubato fashion.

G – the same as F, but with longer basic patterns.

H – very short, rhythmically accented groups of three to five notes, each repeated four to eight times, often associated with a long sequence moving melodic movement up or down a fifth or more.

I – a section of simple metric material with little repetition of rhythmic motifs.

J – a rather complex rhythmic pattern repeated two or more times; the sections named "Kereshmeh" in the radif frequently begin in this fashion.

K – sustained use of a rhythmic ostinato with strong metric organization, such as a chahār mezrāb.

It may be common for an individual gusheh to be dominated by one of these. Normally, however, one hears several of these kinds of rhythmic movements in rather quick succession, each no more than five to ten seconds in length. The general characteristic of the radifs is not their essentially non-metric nature, but their tendency to move quickly from one kind of rhythmic movement to another. The question is to what extent the individual radifs and their components can be distinguished in this way.

First, there is a fundamental difference between the vocal radif of Karimi and the instrumental ones of Boroumand and Ma'roufi. The vocal radif contains far more material with little in the way of rhythmic movement from the beginning of the alphabet in the scheme given below; and indeed, much of its rhythmic structure may, as Tsuge suggests, be based on the rhythmic structure of poetry. The radifs of Ma'roufi and Boroumand differ in one perhaps significant way related to a major difference between the structures of the two.

Boroumand's radif is considerably shorter. Māhour, for example, occupies 40 minutes, in contrast to about 70 minutes for Ma'roufi's Māhour. The number of separately labeled sections is somewhat, but not proportionately, greater in Ma'roufi. Yet, the number of different kinds of rhythmic movement is about the same in a typical section of the two, and perhaps slightly greater in Boroumand. One may conclude from this that Boroumand's radif has a tendency to move more rapidly from one kind of rhythmic movement to another, and that the kind of material which occupies a particular kind of rhythmic movement is elaborated more in Ma'roufi's. At the same time, it seems possible that the rendition of a gusheh in the radif requires a certain amount of change in rhythmic movement, and therefore, if a gusheh is given in brief form, it will change rhythmic type more readily and frequently than a gusheh performed more extensively. Boroumand stays with one kind of rhythm very briefly; Ma'roufi sticks to a pattern or style at considerable length, establishing it thoroughly. This is a typical contrast, found, for example, in the Darāmad group, Dād, and Neshaburak; but not always, as indicated in Table III, in the listing of Delkash.

The classification of rhythmic movement types, as said above, is highly approximate, and sharp lines between them cannot be drawn. Nevertheless, a comparison of the two radifs, Boroumand and Ma'roufi, in terms of the rhythmic movement types used per gusheh, indicates a considerable degree of correspondence. Table III shows that where a gusheh uses predominantly Type A, its analogue in the other radif is likely to follow suit, and so on. The table gives only a few examples from the two radifs, indicating length of the gusheh and, more or less in succession, the types of rhythmic movement used. Where Type H is given, however, this is intended to indicate that it appears occasionally but prominently throughout the gusheh. Where H is not mentioned it nevertheless may appear occasionally, as connecting material and as a way to move from one part of the tonal range to another. Other types used briefly or sporadically are given in parentheses.

Māhour and the other Dastgāhs

One of the fascinating aspects of the Persian radif is the way in which materials from the various dastgāhs are shared. Again using the dastgāh of Māhour as an example, we find that the names of certain gushehs (beyond the generally used names such as darāmad) in Māhour are found also in other dastgāhs. Except for a few instances, the melodic contents of such gushehs are similar. However, we can distinguish degrees of similarity. Greatest resemblance in melodic content appears in the situation in which one master repeats an entire gusheh almost exactly in another dastgāh of his own radif. For example, several gushehs of Māhour also appear in Rāst-Panjgāh, and a few in Navā. Isfahānak appears in all three in Ma'roufi. Somewhat less similarity is found where a gusheh appears in different dastgahs with essentially the same melodic content, but adjusted to a different scale. This is not important in the relationship of Māhour to other dastgāhs, but plays a role in the interrelationship of Chahārgah and Segāh.

A smaller degree of melodic similarity is found where gushehs with the same name share identical beginnings but then diverge. Chahār-pareh in

Table III. Comparison of two Radifs by Type, Length and Rhythmic Movement.

Examples from Dastgāh-e Māhour

	Boroumand			Ma'roufi		
Darāmad group:						
Darāmad	:35 (35 seconds)		DHA	Moghadameh	3:05	BHCK
Kereshmeh	:40		JDE	Koroghli	2:30	IKA
Āvāz	1:30		A (with H and D occ.)	Charār mezrāb	1:00	K
				Bardāsht	:50	A
				Kereshmeh	2:15	JAJA
				Darāmad I	1:25	A
				Darāmad II	1:05	A(G)
				Āvāz	1:35	A
Moqadameh be Dād	:35		D	Dād	2:05	D(H)
Dād	2:15		ADIAHA			
Khosravāni	1:00		DA	Khosravāni	3:00	DHAHA
Delkash	3:20		BABAIAKADBH	Delkash	1:30	CAHDA
				Kereshmeh	:45	JAB
				Chahār mezrāb	:30	K
Neshaburak	1:30		ABDA	Neshaburak	1:55	A

41

Māhour and Abu-Atā in Boroumand's radif is illustrative. There are also some very rare cases in which the melodic content of a single gusheh in Māhour differs completely from that of the identically named gusheh in another dastgāh. Table IV gives examples of some gushehs of Māhour whose names appear also in other dasgāhs.

While the name of a gusheh tends to be associated with a particular piece of melodic material, no matter in whose radif or in what dastgah it appears, there is a tendency for certain characteristic motifs to appear under a variety of names. While a detailed account of this phenomenon must await analysis of all dastgāhs in detail, we can cite at least one example in Māhour. The motif beginning the gusheh Neshaburak in Māhour and Navā appears in the various gushehs named Rāk in Māhour, but also at the beginning of Darāmad of Chahārgāh, Maqlub of Chahārgāh, and at the end of various gushehs in Chahārgāh and Segāh, as well as the beginning of Māyalian in Homāyoun.

A comparative analysis of radifs, even if focused on only dastgah, shows the basic material of Persian music to be a highly complex and intricate network of interrelated units and a separate, related but not identical network of concepts as indicated by names.

We would speculate that examination of a group of radifs from the point of view of content and nomenclature, also taking into account the internal interrelationships of each radif and its component dastgahs, would provide insight into the genesis of this corpus, the way the traditional music system was transmitted, and the way in which it served as a tool for the teaching of improvisation.

Table IV. Gushehs in Māhour also present (by name, not necessarily content) in other dastgāhs. Letters indicate, respectively, the radifs of Boroumand, Karimi, Ma'roufi, and Sabā.

	Shur	Abu Atā	Dashti	Afshāri	Tork	Esfahān	Homāyun	Segāh	Chāhārgāh	Navā	Rāst Panjgāh
Khosravāni					BM						BMS
Neishāburak										BMKS	
Chāhār Pāreh		BMKS									
Feili				K	BKS						
Hesār							MK	BMKS	BMKS		
Neiriz							M				
Shekasteh					BKS						BMKS
Nahib											MKS
Arāq										MKS	M
Mohayyer										M	MKS
Āshur										M	MKS
Basteh Negār		M		B	B			BM	BM	M	S
Esfahānak				K	S	M				M	MS
Hazin	BMK							BM	BM	BMS	MKS
Rāk or its variants											MKS
Majles Afruz	BM										

43

The Four Styles of Notre-Dame Organa
Hans Tischler, *Bloomington, Indiana*

Around 1900, when the repertory of the Parisian organa began to be studied, both the music and the theoretical sources yielded a first approach to the analysis of their style. This approach was brilliantly presented by Friedrich Ludwig in his *Repertorium*.[1] It recognized two general styles, *viz.*, that of organum purum and that of discant. The former was defined as combining a chant tenor or cantus firmus, laid out in notes of differing unmeasured length, often including some very long-held notes, with a duplum of much faster notes, moving in an at least partially free-flowing rhythm. Discant was represented by settings in which both voice parts proceed in a strictly measured rhythm, the tenor normally presenting the chant in either a cantus-planus arrangement of consecutive longs or double longs or in an unchanging rhythmic motif throughout, while the duplum unfolds more or less freely within one of several rhythmic-metric patterns, the so-called modes. According to the witness of Coussemaker's Anonymus IV[2] these two styles could be comfortably connected with the names of two composers, ostensibly associated successively with the cathedral of Notre Dame, Leoninus and Perotinus, who were recognized in their time, the late 12th and early 13th centuries, as the greatest masters of these respective styles.

Whereas the discant style became the ancestor of all succeeding polyphonic music, the organum-purum technique reached its last efflorescence in the Notre-Dame organa, though in conservative provincial centers it lingered on for a long time. It is perhaps most succinctly described in the concluding 13th chapter of Johannes de Garlandia's *De mensurabili musica*,[3] probably the earliest treatise dealing with this repertory. This chapter on *organum in speciali*, *i.e.*, organum in the narrow sense, has been recently analyzed in

---

1. Friedrich Ludwig, *Repertorium Organorum Recentioris et Motetorum Vetustissimi Stili*, vol. I, 1; Halle 1910. New ed. by L.A. Dittmer, New York, Institute of Mediaeval Music, 1964. Ed. of vol. I, 2 and the incomplete vol. II by Friedrich Gennrich, *Summa Musicae Medii Aevi*, vols. 7–8; Langen 1961/62.
2. Edmond de Coussemaker, *Scriptorum de musica medii aevi nova series*, 4 vols.; Paris 1864–76; I, 314f. – Fritz Reckow, *Der Musiktraktat des Anonymus IV*, 2 vols.; Wiesbaden, Franz Steiner, 1967; I,46.— L. A. Dittmer, *Anonymus IV*; New York, Institute of Mediaeval Music, 1959; 36
3. It appears in the redaction of Jerome of Moravia in Coussemaker, *op. cit.*, I, 97–117, and S. M. Cserba, *Hieronymus de Moravia O.P. Tractatus de Musica*, Freiburger Studien zur Musikwissenschaft 2, Regensburg 1935, 294–230, with three unrelated chapters, 14–16, added to the treatise, perhaps by Jerome. See Erich Reimer, *Johannes de Garlandia: De mensurabili musica*, 2 vols.; Wiesbaden, Franz Steiner, 1972.

exemplary fashion by Edward Roesner.[4] Perhaps the most important result of his analysis is the recognition that what Johannes, speaking of the rhythmic flow in the duplum, calls *modus non rectus* designates a free-flowing rhythm within a well defined metric-modal outline, as William Waite had recognized earlier.[5] This recognition gives a firm definition to the style; but it allows for great flexibility of rhythmic interpretation, which a comparative study of the organa clearly reveals.[6]

The discant style is much less problematic. Both parts move within well established metric patterns, which are often rhythmically modified, to be sure, but whose interpretation is greatly aided by the need for harmonic consonance within the contrapuntal context.

Until recently modern scholarship dealt mostly with these two styles and their many problems, although Johannes as well as later theorists also discussed a third style, called copula. But the definition of this style remained nebulous and seemed to find no application in the music. Several writers tried to clarify the meaning of this term, but it was only in 1971 and 1972 that the first comprehensive approach to a definition of this style was made in two publications by Fritz Reckow.[7] It appears that over a period of time the term changed its meaning. In Johannes's treatise it applies to a combination of unmeasured, long-held tenor notes with a strictly rhythmic duplum, which follows one of the modal patterns; in Franco's *Ars cantus mensurabilis*[8] (one of whose copies is included, like Johannes's treatise, in Jerome of Moravia's late thirteenth-century compilation) copula is also described as a sort of cadenza in fast tempo outside of modal rhythm.

Whereas only a few passages in the extant musical sources exemplify this second of Franco's descriptions of the copula, particularly in organa tripla, the style described in Johannes's twelfth chapter appears very often in the repertory. In a recent paper Jeremy Yudkin has clarified the style of the copula further.[9] Indeed, because it has become recognized only recently, this

4. Edward H. Roesner, "Johannes de Garlandia on *Organum in speciali*", paper read at the 47th Annual Meeting of the American Musicological Society, Boston, November 1981.
5. See William G. Waite, *The Rhythm of Twelfth-Century Polyphony*, New Haven, Connecticut, Yale University Press, 1954, 18ff.
6. See Hans Tischler, *The Parisian Two-Part Organa: Complete Comparative Edition*; (forthcoming), New York, Pendragon Press.
7. Fritz Reckow, "Copula" in *Handwörterbuch der musikalischen Terminologie*, Wiesbaden, Franz Steiner, 1971, and *Die Copula*; Mainz, Akademie der Wissenschaften und der Literatur, Wiesbaden, Franz Steiner, 1972.
8. Coussemaker, *op. cit.*, I, 117–136; Cserba, *op. cit.*, 230–259; Gilbert Reaney and André Gilles, *Franconis de Colonia Ars Cantus Mensurabilis*; Corpus Scriptorum de Musica 18, Rome, American Institute of Musicology, 1974.
9. Jeremy Yudkin, "Notre Dame Theory and the Terminology of the Trivium," paper read at the 47th Annual Meeting of the American Musicological Society, Boston, November 1981.

style deserves detailed scrutiny. It may therefore be permitted to repeat and annotate the salient statements about the copula made in Yudkin's paper.

(1) Johannes xii, sentence 2:

...copula dicitur esse id, quod est inter discantum et organum. "Copula is said to be what stands between discant and organum." This statement has been interpreted in two ways: that the copula is stylistically something between discant and organum or that in actual organa it is always placed between a section of organum purum and a discant clausula. Before a decision between these two interpretations can be attempted, it will be necessary to first come to a clearer understanding of how to recognize copulae as differing from either of the other two styles. This clarification is furnished by the next few sentences.

(2) Johannes xii, sentence 3:

... copula est id, quod profertur recto modo aequipollente unisono.

"A copula is performed in strict mode to a long-held note (*unisono*) of equal length."*Modus rectus* here carefully contrasts with *modus non rectus*, applied in chapter xiii to the free-flowing rhythm of organum purum. It is also significant that Johannes employs the term "copula" as applying only to the duplum, exactly as he employs the term *organum in speciali*, as Roesner stressed in his paper, in the next chapter as applying only to the duplum.

(3) Johannes xii, sentences 4–5:

... copula est id, ubicumque fit multitudo punctorum. Punctus... est, ubicumque fit multitudo tractuum.

"A copula contains a number of *puncti*; a *punctus* contains several *tractus*." *Punctus* may be translated in various contexts as note, phrase, or section. Here it is probably best rendered as phrase; Reckow thought of it as "note" and Yudkin better as "section," but meaning what is usually called phrase or period. *Tractus* means a line; Reckow interpreted this to mean the line connecting two notes in a ligature, whereas Yudkin translates *tractus* better as "division line" (between phrases). Although such lines occasionally occur, where a phrase has a feminine ending or where the next phrase begins with an upbeat, the overwhelming majority of such lines indicate rests. Thus Johannes's second definition may be rendered as follows: A copula (usually) contains several phrases; each phrase or period (often) contains several rests (*i.e.*, shorter phrases).

(4) Johannes xii, sentences 6–8:

Et ista pars dividitur in duo aequalia. Unde prima pars dicitur antecedens, secunda vero consequens, et utraque pars continet multitudinem tractuum. Unde tractus fit, ubicumque fit multitudo specierum univoce, ut unisoni aut toni, secundum numerum ordinatum ordine debito.

"And this part (sc. copula) (often) divides into two (approximately) equal portions. The first portion is called antecedent, the second the consequent, and each portion (often) contains several rests. A rest occurs, where there occur a number of well defined (*univoce*) intervals, such as unisons or whole steps, in a well arranged rhythm and a traditional (*debito*) order."

Here three approaches are taken toward defining the copula. The first relates it to the other two styles; the second gives a general definition of its style; the third describes frequent structural aspects of the copula. If we want to grasp its essence, we must start with the second approach. In general, then, a copula consists of a strictly modal duplum above a long-held tenor note (or several such notes). The words with which Johannes casually refers to the tenor, *aequipollente unisono*, are somewhat more extensively treated in the following chapter, the one on *organum in speciali*:

Et eius (sc. organi) aequipollentia tantum se tenet in unisono usque ad finem alicuius puncti, ut secum convenit secundum aliquam concordantiam.

"And its tenor stays on the same tone (*unisono*) until the end of each phrase, as it meets (the duplum) in one of the consonances." As is well established, however, the tenor of organum-purum passages may comprise several long, at any rate unmeasured, notes. Indeed, the word *"convenit"* may well imply a movement of the tenor to another note at the end of a phrase to achieve consonance, a procedure which is quite generally found in both types of settings.

As the third approach then details, often (rather than always, as will be demonstrated below) a copula comprises several such phrases, which are (often) arranged in antecedent-consequent fashion, each normally followed by a rest (or division line). This arrangement usually has two equivalent portions (but sometimes more) which may (or may not) be melodically similar; if they are, they may be composed in ouvert-clos fashion or form a sequence. Several examples of these possibilities are given below. It must be pointed out, however, that these structural possibilities are not unique to copulae but apply equally to portions of organum-purum and discant style.[10]

---

10. See the analysis of the complete repertory in the "Catalogue Raisonné" vol. I, part II, of Tischler, *op. cit.* (see note 6).

They are, therefore, neither a defining nor a delimiting feature of copulae. Johannes' description may well derive from an implicit meaning of the word, deriving from grammar, logic, and rhetoric, which led to the later derivative "couplet," a meaning repeatedly stressed by later theorists cited by Reckow,[11] in connection with ductia and stantipes (Johannes de Grocheo), the sonet (Antonio da Tempo), and the lai *(Règles de la seconde rhétorique)*. But as many passages in the organa prove, Johannes's description of the copula in this regard does not always apply. Thus Franco's examples[12] show that copulae were not necessarily long and could consist of single phrases rather than always offering two or more "coupled" ones. Similarly numerous passages prove that even long copulae do not necessarily contain any melodically equal or similar phrases or may do so only in part.

Therefore the definition of the copula style rests firmly on (2) and (3) above, while (4) adds some descriptive features which as often apply as not and are not specific to this style. The following examples will bear out this statement. Indeed, in many instances short, strictly modal phrases clearly interrupt the limber flow of organum and provide characteristic contrast; not to call such phrases copulae would contradict their stylistic meaning. Nevertheless, to create artistic contrast such phrases must attain a certain minimum length, though it is often difficult to draw a line. To obviate any argument, however, only copulae of substantial length have been chosen here to serve as examples.

Now it is possible to return to the first of Johannes's sentences on the copula, cited above, which has been interpreted to mean that the copula either stands stylistically between organum purum and discant or always appears between a section of organum purum and one of discant. As the musical examples below make clear, the *"inter"* in that sentence must be translated as in style "midway between." In other words, a copula may, but need not always, occur between an organum-purum and a discant setting; just as often it may begin or end a large section or separate two passages of organum-purum or discant style. On the other hand, the copula style clearly stands midway between the other two styles, for it employs a tenor laid out, as in organum purum, in unmeasured, often long-held notes and a duplum in strict modal rhythm like that of a discant clausula.

The three styles described up to here may be tabularly presented as follows:

---

11.   *Cf. Die Copula* (see note 7), 13ff.
12.   *Cf.* the works cited in note 8: Coussemaker, 133; Cserba, 256; Reaney and Gilles, 76f.

	organum purum	copula	discant
duplum:	free-flowing within metric mode	strictly modal	strictly modal
tenor:	unmeasured	unmeasured	strictly measured

This table suggests a fourth stylistic paradigm, *viz.*:

pseudo-discant

duplum:	free-flowing within metric mode
tenor:	strictly measured

This fourth style does, in fact, emerge quite frequently in the organa.[13] Given below are a few examples of this style, which is nowhere mentioned by the theorists and which, like the copula, yet in a second way, stands midway between organum purum and discant.

What remains to be said is that, as in later music, style definition serves a limited goal. A minority of compositions exhibit one or another style throughout or even in smaller segments. Many distant clausulae, *e.g.*, are surrounded by, or begin or end with, phrases of organum purum or copula. Some dissolve the duplum into so many ornaments that they approach pseudo-discant style. Similarly it is often difficult to decide what is meant as organum purum and what represents pseudo-discant, because tenor notes may succeed each other at more or less regular intervals, sometimes as double, triple, or quadruple longs, sometimes intermingling such larger note values with simple longs. In the same manner the demarcation between copula and organum purum passages is often blurred. And it is often a question whether a series of double or quadruple longs in the tenor qualify a passage as a clausula, a copula, or pseudo-discant (see Exs. 2d, 3). To state the facts clearly: the four styles analyzed above represent ideal types, which, like such terms as sonata-form or rondo, appear in living music in multiple individual manifestations, which more often than not depart from the "pure" or ideal types.

---

13.   *Cf.* note 10.

Music Examples*

(1a) Copula without melodic repetition, between two organum-purum passages; the first of the latter including varied sequences: M 16, II–III F, *Alleluya. Nonne cor* (V), f. 110v

(1b) Copula with double period structure and cadence, 2nd period ouvert-clos with variation, between two clausulae: M 57, IV–VI F, *Alleluya. Benedictus es* (V), f. 143v–144

*   In the examples accidentals given in the manuscripts are shown in the staff; they are shown in parentheses, when continued from previously given accidentals, and above notes, in parentheses, where editorial. Short oblique bars above notes indicate *currentes*.

(1c) Copula without melodic repetition, at beginning of an organum: 01, I F (W1, W2), *Iudea et Iherusalem* (R), f. 65

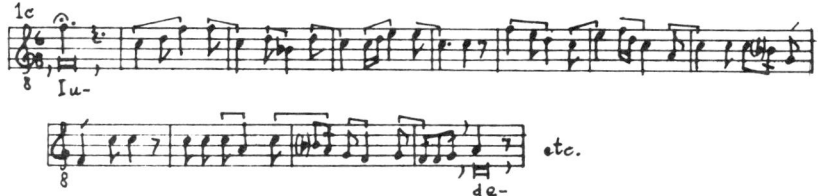

(1d) Copula with sequence, at end of an organum: M 39, VI F (W 1, W 2), *Alleluya. In conspectu* (V), f. 131

(1e) Short copula without melodic repetition, contrasting with organum-purum-passage: 04, I F, *In columbe* (R), f. 67v

(2a) Sequence in organum purum: 020, I F, *Maria* (R), f. 77v

(2b) Sequence in pseudo-discant: M 44, II W 2, *Alleluya. Hic Martinus* (V), f. 80

(2c) Sequence in a discant clausula: *Domino* 3, F, f. 88v

(2d) Sequence above regular long note values; organum purum, pseudo-discant or clausula? : M 8, III W 1, *Laus tua* (V), f. 24v

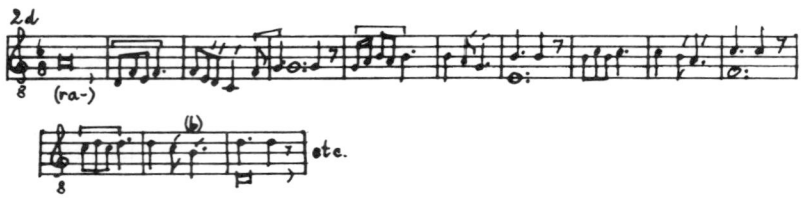

(2e) Sequences in pseudo-discant above an irregularly moving tenor: M 8, II F (W1, W2), *Laus tua* (V), f. 104v

(3) Clausula or copula?, with initial and final flourish: M 47, IV F, *Posuisti* (V), f. 136v

The Glee: the Term and its Connotation[1]
An Annotated Documentation

Herzl Shmueli, *Tel-Aviv*

The glee as a musical genre served English composers for over two hundred years, from the middle of the 17th until nearly the end of the 19th century. The latter part of the 18th witnessed its development and progress well into the twenties of the following century, during which it reached and maintained its eminence. It then gradually declined until it disappeared as a living musical form in the course of a few decades.

Notwithstanding the continuous period during which glees were being produced in England, and the impressive repertoire that resulted,[2] historians of Western music – including the English – have tended to approach the subject with indifference or neglect. One of the most likely reasons for this attitude could be ascribed to the lack of clarity which exists with regard to the nature and quality of the glee.

To this may be added the fact that since its flowering, but even more so during its decline, professional as well as amateur musicians held ambivalent attitudes as to the use of the term "glee" for different musical compositions – attitudes ranging from absolute denial of its application to a specific work (irrespective of its designation as such by the composer), to the unquestioning labelling as such of works with varied techniques and construction.

Despite such contradictary attitudes the glee was, in fact, important in the history of English music, playing a prominent social role, and serving as a source of pride during long barren stretches in English musical composition.

The glee, at its height, was a product of the union of social drives with the need for musical-artistic self-expression, with the social motivations counterbalancing the artistic, and at times, outweighing them.

The purpose of this study, then, is to examine the socio-musical background of the glee at closer range, mainly during its flourishing. In attempting to present a well-rounded picture of the subject, reference has been made to the thoughts and attitudes of contemporaries – their approval,

---

1. This article forms part of a larger work dealing with the relations and interactions of English music and the music of the Continent during the period known rather controversially as "The Early Romantic Era" (approximately the last decade of the 18th and the first three of four decades of the 19th centuries).
2. BARRETT: 1886: *"It is calculated that nearly 25,000 glees have been published. It would be impossible to reckon the number to those that remain in manuscript"* (p. 333).

enthusiasm or reservations published at the time, their appreciation or critical views of the composers and their works, as both active participants and as audience.

The "glee"[3] is characterized by *Grove's Dictionary* (1980 edition) as *a simply harmonized composition for three or more voices (originally male) without accompaniment.* The earlier 1927/28 edition mentioned also that glees were performed by *solo voices, usually those of men.* We may add that, during its lifetime, an instrumental accompaniment was sometimes added, and that glees could even be rendered with an orchestral accompaniment in concert form.

At any rate, there are no set rules or guidelines to which the glee *must* adhere. The length of the compositions can consist of a few bars or of many pages; the form may vary from one simple movement to far greater complexity.

As to their execution, they can be rendered by solo voices only as well as by a choir, or by solo voices and choir; generally they are for male voices, but some glees include participation of women's voices as well. As to the textual contents – it is impossible to determine any common direction or factors, and the words seem to be a matter of free choice on the part of the composer.

This lack of unity among known glees makes it impossible to arrive at a short explanation or definition of their basic character. But one may venture to say that part of the charm of the glee lies precisely in its lack of "discipline" and in its not being confined by an *a priori* definition.

Some further explanations of the term glee appear in other English commentaries. According to BARRETT: 1886, the glee is a kind of musical sonnet in which the poetical idea, suggested *"in the opening phrase, is continued and intensified by every subsequent expression, until the peak is reached in the final phrases, and the beauty of the imagery culminates in some exquisite application of the motto of the whole..."* (p. 64);

"Alternate passages, lively and slow, to suit the sentiment of the words, are the rudiments of those contrasted movements which were to form one of the distinguished features of the glee" (p. 211).

3. *"From the Anglo-saxon glíw or gléo, 'entertainment'; in particular 'musical entertainment' and hence 'music'."* It should be stressed that although the word "glee", as it is used at present in modern spoken English, denotes "gay" or "gaiety" and derives from the same source as the musical term, it has little relevance to the texts of the musical "glee", which may indeed be a work full of gaiety, but which may also convey a wider range of feelings. Hence there are glees of various categories, which according to their characters can be described as convivial, cheerful, humorous, pastoral, Bacchanalian, elegiac, serious and even comic.

DAVEY: 1921 adds that the glee is *"set throughout, the music not being repeated to successive stanzas..."* (p. 376).

"Glee differs from the madrigal mainly in being intended to specially display solo voices; madrigals are best sung by a chorus (ibid.)

WALKER: 1945 explains more precisely: *"The glee indeed was a compromise: it was more definitely melodious and rhythmical than the madrigal and more especially laid out for solo male voices, while at the same time it preserved the artistic interests of more or less continuous rather than strophic design and a certain amount of contrapuntal elaboration, as well as the homogeneity of tone resulting from the absence of accompaniment"* (pp. 236–237).

The above comments relate to the general nature of the glee and cover a period of one hundred years from Barrett: 1886 to Grove: 1980. Our study, however, is concentrating on the fifty years beginning with the last quarter of the 18th through the first quarter of the 19th century.

The principal element which all glees had in common at that time was that they included at least three voices. Nevertheless there were occasions when the work was written for more voices, and to the same extent we come across works for a chorus which are also called glees, works for chorus and soloists, works with the accompaniment of one or even two pianos, with an orchestral accompaniment, and works intended to be performed responsorially. And even the "masculinity" of execution by male voices could also be questioned at that time, as there were a few glees written solely for female voices.

Another common feature – with very few exceptions – was the harmonic texture of the glees at this time. The "simply harmonized composition" (Grove: 1927/28), is generally applicable, though here and there we come across a sort of "contrapuntal" work; but in such cases the polyphony is generally weak and disappears eventually in the overall harmony.

In these two factors – that of being written for at least three voices, and in their harmonic textures – lie the only kindred features of the glee during that period. One cannot find any other common element – neither in their length, structure nor in the texts. With very few exceptions, we could find little supporting evidence to Barrett's remarks (1886:5):

"... the poetical idea, suggested in the opening phrase, is continued and intensified by every subsequent expression..."

"... alternate passages, lively and slow, to suit the sentiment of the words, are the rudiments of those contrasted movements".

As to the "continuity" of the glee ("set throughout") of which Davey speaks, and the "more or less continuous rather that strophic design," as

Walker puts it, there is actually no evidence of this during the period under discussion.

Summarizing to this point: *During the period between the last quarter of the 18th and the first of the 19th centuries, the term "glee" could be applied to any vocal work with a secular text, or any vocal piece which stands on its own, within a larger whole (such as a piece within an opera), which is written for three or more voice-parts without any specification regarding the musical texture (harmonic, contrapuntal or a combination of both), the verbal contents, the length or the structure.*

During the years of its popularity, the glee lost its basic connotation as being intended, in principle, for three or more male solo voices without accompaniment. An examination of the sources leads us to understand that even from its outset, the use of the term "glee" to describe a musical form (and it appears as such in the sources) was decidely unclear.

To the best of my knowledge, the term "glee" appeared in a musical context for the first time in 1652, in a collection of works published by John Playford (1623–ca.1686): *Select Musicall Ayres and Dialogues*, which includes a piece by Charles Coleman (d. 1644) "To Bacchus, we to Bacchus sing" and is described as a *"Glee with chorus for three voices"*. Fifteen years later, in 1667, in the second volume of *The Musical Companion*,[4] we find *"Dialogues, Glees, Ballads and Ayres for 2, 3, and 4 voices"*.

A study of the glees in this early material does not reveal any common musical features apart from a similarity in the verbal contents, for the glees in the *Musical Companion* are all devoted to the pleasures of eating and drinking. However, this subject as the sole contents of the texts does not figure in glees written after this period.

It was only during the course of the hundred years from the birth of the glee up until its flourishing era, that it fits, to a certain extent, the characterisation of being written for three or more unaccompanied voices. Among the composers who lent themselves to writing glees as described here were Henry Purcell (1659–1695), John Blow (1648–1708), Michael Wise (ca.1648–1687) and John Playford (1623–ca.1686).

As to the origins of the glee, not only do the commentators disagree, but even in the words of one and the same there are sometimes frequent changes and contradictions. BARRETT: 1866, *e.g.*, remarks (p. 62) that the musical form of *the Catch*, in which Purcell excelled, *was the immediate precursor of the Glee*, but continues that it was *foreshadowed in the musical treatment of certain Villanelli*. Furthermore, he informs us (p. 143) that *the madrigal "The*

---

4. A collection also published by John Playford.

Silver Swan" of Gibbons is usually regarded as the prototype of a glee. Referring to the time around 1700, the author designates *the Round, the Catch, and the Canon* as *the immediate precursors of the glee*.

In contrast with these bewildering statements, the commentators of the last quarter of the 18th and the first quarter of the 19th centuries are of the almost unanimous opinion that the glee was derived from the madrigal.

The Quarterly Musical Magazine and Review, the first British musical periodical published between 1818 and 1829, explains (all the italics in the following citations are the author's):

1. The English glee is *clearly derived from the madrigal*, which was only a modification of the ecclesiastical style of composition that prevailed when the madrigal was in vogue. *Glees, therefore, savour more of the church than of the theatre*. This may be observed even in the most cheerful. – QMM 3 (1821): 472.

2. The succession of amusement derived from catches, madrigals and glees appears to have been slightly interrupted by the *brief and casual introduction of the viols* as assistant to the voice in the *performance of madrigals*, and perhaps it may be in a measure owing to the fact that the too generally artificial construction of madrigals, thereby injuring or lowering the expression of passion, made this defect more apparent, and led *to the substitution of glees*. – QMM 4 (1822): 364.

The first musical monthly in Britain, *The Harmonicon* (1823–1833), successively expresses similar opinions:

3. *The Glee is the offspring of the madrigal*, and the madrigal owes its birth to the *motet*: *the church is the parent of them all*, and is accused, by those who have no relish to English harmony, of having *transmitted her gravity and gloom* to her latest musical descendant. Such persons usually *apply the term psalmody to glees*... – H 5 (1827): 65.

4. *Glees... whose parentage may certainly be traced to the madrigal*, a produce of foreign origin, but once cultivated in this country with so much skill as to rival if not exceed the best specimen that the Netherlands and Italy in their proudest days were able to furnish. – H 10 (1832): 174.

But we may find other opinions as well: *The Musical World* (weekly, 1836–1891) declares:

5. The glee is *so distinct from the madrigal* in its spirit, and in the style of its construction that we would not say, with the writer in the *Athenaeum*,[5] *"it is but a madrigal diluted"* – no more than we would say of ale, it is but brandy diluted. Let it be confessed, that *a glee is no madrigal at all, but only a glee:*. – "Fleas are not lobsters, d--n their souls" – MW 11 (1839):80.

The Golden Age of the glee is represented by one generation of composers, including John Callcott (1766–1821), Robert Cooke (1768–1814), William Crotch (1775–1847), John Davy (1763–1824), Thomas Greatorex (1758–1831), William Horsley (1774–1858), William Knyvett (1779–1856), William Linley (1767–1835), Sir John Andrew Stevenson (1761–1833), Samuel Wesley (1766–1825), and Samuel Webbe Sr. (1740–1816).

5. A weekly; appeared from 1833 to 1868.

Youth of the Gloomy Brow.

(from Ossian)

a Glee for 3 Voices,

Composed by

Dr. CALLCOTT.

Pr. 1s. 6d.

LONDON. Printed for G. WALKER, at his Music Warehouse 106 Gt. Portland Street.

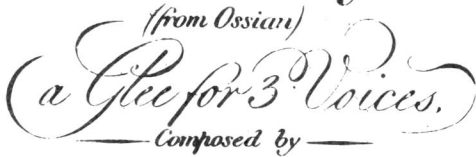

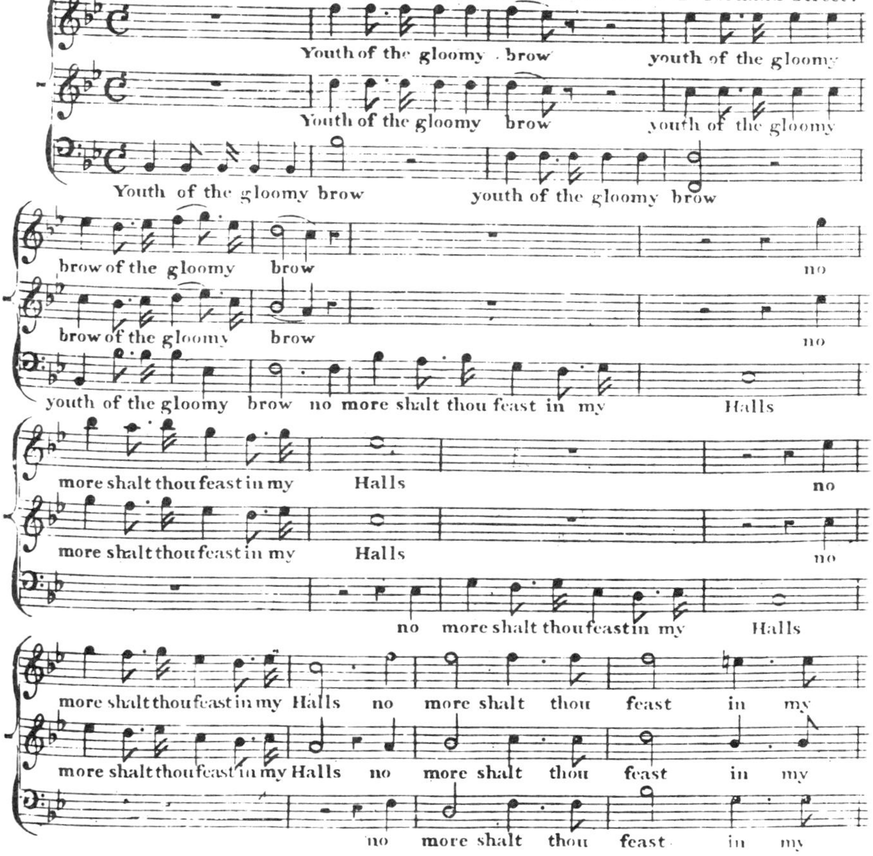

Samuel Webbe, the man who raised the glee to its artistic peak, died in 1816, the year which actually marks the beginning of the decline of this musical form. Despite the large number of glees produced after this, there are very few outstanding works among them. The waning of the glee lasted for some decades and it finally ceased altogether before the 19th century drew to a close.

The fact that the usage of the term "glee" is frequently inapt can be understood from the writings of the period. Knowledgeable commentators repeatedly opposed the use of the term whenever the work referred to seemed unworthy of or unsuitable to this description. They advocated a different approach and did not hesitate to say so whenever the occasion arose. At the other extreme, however, there were those who applied the term "glee" indiscriminately, without discerning the changes and variations that had taken place in the subject itself. From the same sources, which cover a number of decades, we can assume that their contesting efforts were in vain. The composers and the public held their ground and continued to use the term glee for a multitude of varied compositions, providing that these contained more than two singing parts.

It would be helpful, at this point, to corroborate what has been said until now, by bringing forward, in their own words, some comments from these sources. All this supportive material, without exception, is gleaned from the professional literature of the period, mainly from already-mentioned periodicals dealing with music. These journals contained readers' and editors' reactions to newly-published compositions and to their performances, as well as comments on musical matters in general, particularly in England.

Through a closer study of these sources and an examination of the authenticity of the works we have cited, a clear and vivid picture of musical life at the time emerges, and with it, an elucidation of the glee.

We should first emphasize the degree of pride shown by the English in being the sole *possessors* of the glee. This is an important point, as we are referring to a period of aridity in original English musical creation (to which the writers in question admit, in one way or another).

According to the sources mentioned, the glee stands out brightly within this twilight, and it is proudly spoken of as "ours and ours alone," and as a work "not to be ashamed of;" the glee reveals all that is genial and excellent in the Englishman: The gentility and spiritual and emotional balance which are typical of the people of these isles.

The following are a number of passages which serve as witness to this national pride:

6. These are the qualities [of the glee] which appear to us to make it so peculiarly national, so peculiarly English. The construction completely harmonizes with the caste, tender, mild and gentle, yet warm and true expression of passion, banishing all extravagance, congenial to the English delicacy, yet not wanting the English strength and depth of feeling – QMM 4 (1822): 366.

7. The *claims to originality* set up by English composers who have lived within the *last half century* have mainly rested upon that *species of writing* we call glees. – QMM 6 (1824): 87.

8. ...glees, a species of composition which we can certainly *boast of as indigenous to our own soil*.– H 4(1826): 199.

9. [the glee is] a species of music, which may with strictness be termed *national* – H 5 (1827): 11.

10. The true glee... is... *a native of England* and has hitherto been *confined to its parent soil*. H 8(1830): 432.

11. ... glees, justly styled *superior English composition*... – H 8 (1830): 51

12. The glee is *our national music*, is *indigenous to these islands, and a beautiful species of composition however viewed*. – H 11 (1833): 148

13. ...that truly English species of composition called a Glee... and *our national pride is gratified*, when we reflect on the many admirable works of this kind. – H 11 (1833): 143.

14. ... the Glee... as a plant of native growth; has hitherto been *cherished with a jealous care by* our English musicians, and made their chief resource. – MW 11 (1839): 80

Here are further indications of the special qualities ascribed to the glee:

15. The genius of English musicians has in no species of writing manifested more fire, force and sweetness, even should we hesitate to allow their *strong claim to originality*, than in the composition of *part-songs*, or, as they are now *more generally called, Glees.* – QMM 2 (1820: 107.

16. For if there are any species of composition in which our *native musicians have particularly excelled*, it is in the Glee. – QMM 3 (1821): 366.

17. Glees, indeed, are the peculiar delight of all Englishmen, who have a real taste for music. They are identified with our tastes, manners and habits, and... they exert influence over us, which is not often exerted by more elaborate and artificial compositions. – QMM 3 (1821): 472

18. [The Glees and their composers]... claim the station which they *unquestionably hold in the musical world*. – QMM 5 (1823): 16.

19. I have... lately seen a collection of glees... which for *beauty* and *simplicity* may be justly styled *superior English compositions*. – H 8 (1830): 51.

It is worth noting that in seven of the fourteen immediately foregoing passages, the writers use the expressions: "species of writing," "species of composition," "species of music," when speaking of the glee. There are also instances of the word "style" being used instead of "species":

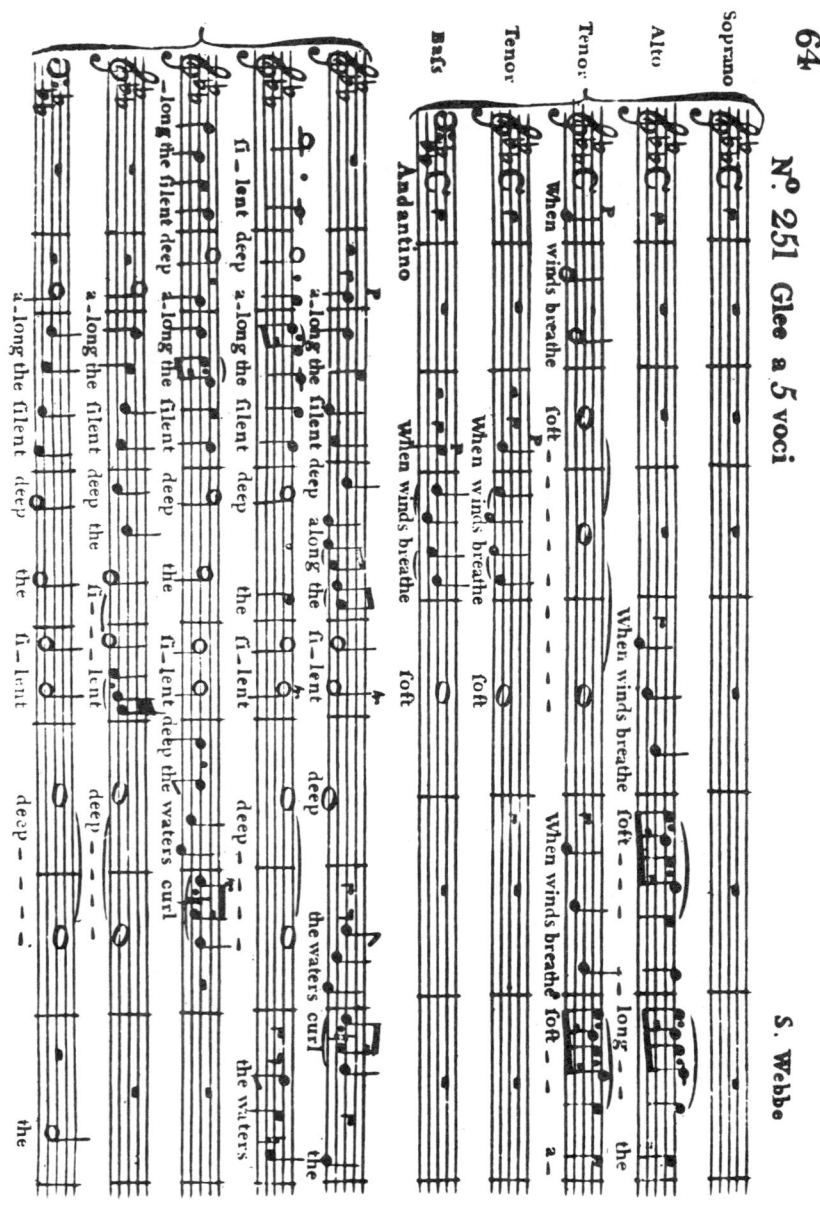

20. ...that *style* which was brought to *such perfection* by Cooke, Webbe..., the worthy successors of these admirable madrigalists... – H 2 (1824): 24.

21. ...that truly English *style* of music, the *glee*... – H 4 (1826): 157.

Many writers claim simplicity as one of the glee's highest virtues. Thus in passage 9, for example, we have, "which for beauty and simplicity may be justly styled superior English composition," and, indirectly in passage 17, when speaking of the influence of the glee on the English: "they exert an influence over us, which is not often exerted by more elaborate and artificial compositions."

It is difficult to free oneself from the provincialism that issues from this overemphasis on simplicity, especially when the author of passage 17 does not hesitate to refer to more *elaborate* and *artificial* compositions.

The "originality" of the glee also calls for some comment. Whereas in passage 15, written in 1820, the writer uses elegant terms to present his reservations regarding the "originality" of the glee: "even should we hesitate to allow their strong claim for originality," the author of passage 7, from 1824, leaving personal opinions aside, offers those of the composers on this subject: "The claims to originality set up by English composers... have mainly rested upon... glees."

Let us return to passages 20 and 21 above.

The authors of these passages do not explain what they mean by their use of the word 'style'. As far as they are concerned, however, it seems that there is no need to spell out their use of this term, for they are confirmed in their opinions that certain qualities are inimical to the "true" glee and that these are identical with the basic character of the English. It is therefore self-evident that "Englishness" is the style of the glee; when these qualities are not present in a composition, it is not a glee – at any rate, not a *genuine* glee.

Accordingly, the writers discuss the various aspects of the personality and character of the composers, and if these are not consistent with their requirements, then naturally the outcome could not be a *genuine* glee. In some of the foregoing passages, there are indications of this, and at times, more than an indication (see, for instance, passages 6 to 17).

One of the basic qualities required is an *emotional and spiritual balance*, a lack of extremism in expression "banishing all extravagance, congenial to English delicacy" as it is put in passage 6 and elaborated on in the following passages:

22. The legitimate subjects for glees are *sentiments abstracted* as much *as possible from character*... Wherever the sentiment is mingled with specific character it ceases to be a glee – it

becomes a *dramatic trio* or *quartetto*... a something but not a glee. – QMM 4 (1822): 365.

The same writer continues with both good and bad examples of his concept of the glee:

23. Thus, for instance, we should exclude Dr. Callcott's "Red-cross Knight," Reeves's "Oh who had seen the miller's wife" and Moore's "O lady fair" from the list of glees. *They are musical dramatic dialogues or scenes, but not glees.* – QMM 4 (1822): 365.

On the other hand:

24. "By Celia's Arbor" a glee by Horsley, and "How sweet, how fresh" by Paxton, *breathe all the fervency of love, without any distinct idea of the lover being affixed.* – QMM 4 (1822): 365

And on no condition should one get personal:

25. "See the chariot at hand here of love", (Horsley) and "Crabbed age and youth", (Stevens), *awake the lighter fires without conveying any absolute notion of the individual.* – QMM 4 (1822): 365.

26. "Wine does wonders", (Eccles) and "Life's a bumper", (Wainwright) fill the mind with all the joviality of the table, yet none of these can we assign more than a *general character*. – QMM 4 (1822): 365–366.

27. ...the glee... demands a *chasteness* and *severity of style*, which is quite characteristic, and which is *entirely destroyed by any passage of dramatic cast.*

Whatever the subject, however airy its treatment, this solidity, this *intrinsic dignity of manner*, appears to our judgment to be a sine qua non.... pieces whose construction is so exceedingly light and simple [do not] reach the character of the glee. – QMM 9 (1827): 119.

28. For a *glee cannot rise above a certain mark of expression*, and always fails in attending to do so... We seem to require of a [Glee] composer, that he should be of a *certain healthful and even temper of mind, not over-passionate perhaps, yet with his feelings whole* and well-proportioned; gifted with a quick sense of the pleasurably and the hearty, and with a natural bias towards the smiling side of things; and, *when serious of complaining, rather yielding softly under the pressure of calamity than either passionately bewailing it of rising above it.* – MW 11 (1839): 81.

29. Graceful and expressive melody, pure harmony and modulation carefully studied and conducted, are the elements, which compose the really fine glee; when such music is united to the poetry of our greatest authors, it is not astonishing that it should possess a charm for unsophisticated minds, of which many other species of composition cannot boast. – QMM 3 (1821): 472.

In other words, the identification of a composition as to whether or not it is a glee lies in its essentially bearing certain characteristics of the English, who express themselves musically in this form.

As to the musical expression itself and its various components, such as the melody, the harmony, the rhythm, the counterpoint, the structure and the text – for all these one cannot find any mandatory approach, just as one cannot find any common features in the works themselves during the period referred to, apart from the harmonic texture, which almost completely dominates the glee of that time.

From the above, we arrive at the conclusion that the extra-musical elements, such as certain human traits, national character as well as social position, played a large part in the contemporary evaluation of the glee, sometimes even a larger part than the musical and professional aspects.

The glee was given considerable momentum by the many singing clubs that were springing up from the middle of the 18th century. At these clubs the members (generally some fifty to a hundred) met regularly for their mutual entertainment: to eat, drink and converse on topics of the day, to smoke and enjoy the friendly atmosphere, the very peak of which was achieved by communal singing.

The commissioning of new works was part of the order of the day, and a very significant number of compositions resulted. Many clubs offered prizes for works they considered outstanding.

The glee, as one of the musical forms in greatest demand at the clubs, made its way from the clubs to the outside world and the general public. At first, the music-loving club members hailed from the upper classes and were joined by well-known professionals, but in a relatively short time, the instititution of singing clubs spread to a much wider society. All the members were expected to participate in the singing, which called for a certain familiarity in reading scores, but there were also instances of "passive" members being accepted, who merely came to listen, but took part in all the other activities with gusto.

The following were some of the most active clubs:

The *Noblemen's and Gentlemen's Catch Club*[6] which was established in London in 1761 and whose stated aims were "the improvement of vocal harmony" and the "encouragement of the composition and performances of canons, catches and glees." One should not be misled by the name "Catch Club" – glees were there as popular as catches, and sometimes more so. In 1766, the *Anacreontic Society* was set up, also in London, and its members met "for supper and the singing of catches, glees and songs." The *Canterbury Catch and Glee Club* was formed in 1779 and the *Glee Club of London* in 1787.

Many more clubs were set up in London and elsewhere around the country, even during the decline of the glee; partly out of inertia and partly

---

6. Another society established in London during the first half of the century, in 1741, but not for the purpose of singing glees and catches was "The Madrigal Society".

with intention of renewing and reviving the good old days, but these did not do much to stop the process of deterioration and eventually the disappearance of the glee.

Some of these were: *The Melodists Club*; *The Manchester Gentleman's Glee Club*; *Oldham Glee Club*; *The Abbey Glee Club*. The latter, according to the announcement of its establishment, stated as its aims: *"The Abbey Glee Club... has been established by several members of the choir at Westminster Abbey, with the praiseworthy intention of affording encouragement to young glee writers, and singers, and thus bringing them and their works more readily before the public...."*. – MW 17 (1842): 133.

As an example of the seriousness with which the members treated the setting up of these societies, we cite from the Rules of the *Noblemen's and Gentlemen's Catch Club*, as they were published anew in 1808 and printed in MWW 2 in 1820, pp. 327–328.

30. The club is still held at the Thatched House, and their meetings commence the Tuesday nearest January 18, and continue till the Tuesday nearest the 4th of June. *Every member of the club must be able to sing his part in a catch or glee,* and *the custom is to call on each person at table from right to left.* The high rank and respectability of the members of this society renders it exceedingly private and difficult of access. *The following are the laws of its government:...*

In the following twelve paragraphs of the Rules, rigorous "penal laws" are set up according to which the members were obliged to pay for every offence against the rules. Even an increase of income was taxed with the half of one percent.

As to the convivial atmosphere of these clubs, the following poem which appeared in 1830, still convinces us of the easygoing circumstances, replete with the charm of friendship and feeling of 'togetherness' as well as a note of nostalgia, which prevailed. – H 8 (1830): 503.

31. When friends are met o'er merry cheer,
   And laughing eyes are laughing near,
   And in the goblet's bosom clear
   The cares of day are drown'd;
   When puns are made and bumpers quaff'd,
   And mild Wit shoots his roving shaft,
   And Mirth his jovial laugh had laugh'd,
   Then is our banquet crown'd
   Ah gay, ah gay
   Then is our banquet crown'd.

When *glees* are sung and *catches* troll'd
And bashfulness grows bright and bold,
And Beauty is no longer cold,
And Age no longer dull;
When chimes are brief and cocks do crow
To tell us it is time to go-
Yet how to part we do not know-
Then is our feast at full!
Ah gay, ah gay,
Then is our feast at full!

As already pointed out, many of the glees found their way from the clubs to the general public. Since 1761, the year in which the *Noblemen's and Gentlemen's Catch Club* was founded, there were signs of an ever-growing tendency to perform glees at public concerts and private homes, and this inclination continued for some decades in the nineteenth century. One can say that the time at which the glee reached its eminence, was also the period in which it reached its largest public.

In addition, from the moment the glee was freed from the social confinement of the clubs, composers of the glee found new directions for this form which would attract the general public. Understandably, changes and variations would be called for and the inclusion of instruments, in addition to voices, was but one change. With all these modifications and innovations, or perhaps despite them, the term glee was still applied.

We shall now quote some contemporaries who fell into two camps: one which denied the use of the term 'glee' when the work did not appear to them to have the character of a 'glee', and the other which used the term when referring to works of exceedingly varied nature and compositional techniques.

32. A pretty, entertaining *opera*, named Maid Marian [by Mr. Bishop], was brought out at this theatre [Covent Garden]... it abounds very much in *glees* and other pieces for many voices."

It should be pointed out that the glees which were performed in an operatic framework were done so with orchestral accompaniment.

33. This four-voiced *glee*... is written for a countra-tenor [sic], two tenors and a bass, and anywhere but upon the stage, [speaking of an opera, in this case] would be improved by the *omission* of the accompaniment. – H 1 (1823): 26.

34. Mr. Parry's is a very pretty *lady's glee*, easy to sing, airy... – H 4 (1826): 226.

And now we have the remarks of those who were willing to "compromise" and accepted the term glee for all manner of compositions:

35. [In Bishop's opera, "The Maid of Milan"], a *Serenade* for four men's voices... which is popular, because all music of the *Glee-species is now in great request at the theatres* – H 1 (1823): 128.

36. [this glee] is a delightful *sestetto*, with a musical phrase, or sequence, running through it – a kind of burden. – H 1 (1823): 27.

37. This ... *popular air is well harmonized by*... *and converted into a very pleasant trio, a glee.* – H 3 (1825): 159.

38. The charming *glee*, as it was to be turned into a *chorus*, might, fitly enough, be previously made a *quintett* of, but we like the old adage, let well alone: there is *rich simplicity* in the *original three-part glee*, which seems to say *noli me tangere*. – H 4 (1826): 127–128.

The writer of the above passage 38 does not object to the use of the term glee, whether it is after being arranged for a chorus or a quintet, but he prefers the simplicity of the three-voice-part original.

In the following passage from a review of a new collection of glees, the author goes so far as to apply the term glee to parts of a composition by a non-English composer who was probably not even aware of his writing "glees": –

39. ... in some of Rossini's operas, a strong disposition to try on it the effect of transplantation is very obvious, for *what are those vocal unaccompanied pieces* for three or more voices, and in which that composer seems with reason to have placed great reliance, *but glees of one movement?* – H 8 (1830): 432.

It goes without saying that any movement to suit creative expression to the tastes of the general public will result in a lowering of artistic standards to some degree – and glees were not an exception to this levelling process.

Some passages in this vein follow:

40. All music of the Glee-species is now in great request at the theatres, We cannot in any other way account for the applause that it receives, for it *contains nothing new."* – H 1 (1823): 129.

41. Let it not be thought that we here mean to ridicule or disparage that truly English species of composition called a Glee;... We only wish to deter industrious professors from wasting their time by showing them how much has been thrown away by those who have not taken an exact measure of their ability. *For it is so easy in glee-writing to approach very near to mediocrity*, which people, blinded by self-love, mistake for excellence, that many are induced to compose who, when too late, are taught, by being neglected, that they have never felt the inspirations of genius...

We are not without some very able glee composers at the present moment... but the number is very small... – H 1 (1823): 143.

42. ...Such [is] indeed the history of the majority of glees, of which *not five in a hundred are destined to survive* a very few forced performances. – H 7 (1829): 46.

43. ...It is too commonly the habit of modern glee-writers to speak of such compositions as if they were addressed to the eye rather than to the ear. They are too apt to neglect melody and to consider harmony the best which appears best on paper... and whose compositions, when published, fall dead from the press without the slightest chance of resuscitation... – H 10 (1832): 174.

44. ...The glees have been much overrated... they are species of composition affording remarkable facilities to mediocrity... they require to be very good, and are yet often very bad indeed. ... Let us admit that it is a composition of another, and no doubt, a lower grade [than the madrigal], but possessed of its proper beauties, and with a style.... of sufficiently marked individual excellence.

...We know what glees *ought* to be, because we have seen what they *have been*: if in the mean time we are disgusted by innumerable second-rate compositions called glees – miserable, poverty-stricken things, that label the good name they inherit – is it quite fair to reverse the divine vengeance – to visit the sins of the offspring on the parent? – MW 11 (1839): 80.

45. Some of the best composers are destitute of his [Webbe's] excellence; they attempt a complicated style, thinking that, as objects look larger in a mist, their compositions will swell out into gigantic proportions...

We often say in reference to others that this *glee would be well if curtailed or that that glee begins well but ends feebly.* – MW 11 (1839): 82.

Further echoes of this attitude can be found in the following passages, in which there is the tendency to place the blame for the decline of the glee on foreign influences which infiltrated into England or on the 'over-popularisation' of the glee, or in other words, the gradual eradication of the glee during the years.

46. "Demand creates supply" is a maxim in commerce, and if we apply it to the commerce of music, it appears to be obvious by the *paucity of English glees published*, that the decline of encouragement extended to English music is not exaggerated... But we are unwilling that this sound and wholesome English taste should decay, if any efforts of ours can stay the progress of its decline or recall the patronage that now so decidedly, we fear, is *wandering towards foreign music*. – QMM 3 (1821): 366.

47. ...the kind of music [Glee] is charming per se, and only *fell into neglect* here *from excessive use* ... till satiety necessarily ensued: what in moderation had been delightful, in excess proved intolerable, and our native plant ceased to be cultivated. – H 8 (1830): 432.

48. ... the fashionable influenza – a malady, which prevails to a considerable extent in this country – *that of admiring only foreign music*.

Some people think it a degradation to acknowledge any acquaintance with works of those genuine English composers..., while Rossini, Pacini, Nicolini, and every other ini, absorb all their admiration...

Under such discouraging circumstances how we wonder at the death of English composers? Still there are a few who, in spite of the unpopularity of English music, continue to compose, particularly songs and *glees*. – H 8 (1830): 51.

[On the Yorkshire Grand Music Festival]

49. ... If we might demur in the slightest degree, it would be to the too numerous *concerted pieces*, *glees*, in particular, which would be replaced with much interest by Solos... – H 1 (1823): 151.

The significance of the Glee lies in its being the result of the union of social motivations with the need for musical-artistic self-expression, a union, which was not always in favour of the artistic element. But in spite of the social motivation sometimes outweighing the artistic one, a rich repertoire of glees reached musical-artistic heights, winning the pride of Englishmen.

The struggle between pride on one side, and doubts as to the "value" of the glee on the other side, combine to make this musical form so touchingly human.

Abbreviations

BARRET 1886	Barret, W. Alexander, *English Glees and Part Songs*. London, 1886.
DAVEY 1921	Davey, Henry, History of English Music. 2nd edition, London, 1921.
H	*The Harmonicon*. London, 1823–1838.
MW	*The Musical World*. London, 18367–1891.
QMM	*The Quarterly Musical Magazine and Review*. London, 1818–1829.
WALKER 1945	Walker, Ernest, *A History of Music in England*. London, 1907; reprint 1945.

Invention Individuelle et Tradition Collective dans la Musique Juive de Hongrie*

Judit Frigyesi, *Philadelphia*

Dans les communautés juives de Hongrie, appartenant toutes à la culture achkénaze, on voit se rencontrer et se confondre les deux branches du judaïsme est-européen, notamment les traditions polono-lithuano-russe et allemande. Dans le matériel hongrois, on peut découvrir les traces de ces deux traditions constituant un répertoire très varié par régions. L'influence la plus forte du style allemand est sensible dans la région de la ville de Pozsony (Presbourg, auj. Bratislava, Tchécoslovaquie) qui possédait une culture mixte contenant des éléments slaves, hongrois et allemands. C'est le territoire de la Subkarpathie (Hongrie du Nord-Est) qui était le plus influencé par le judaïsme polonais, plus précisément celui de la Galicie. Certaines villes de cette région comme Munkács (Moukatchevo), Nagyszöllös (Vinogradov), Beregszász (Beregovo), Ungvár (Oujgorod, auj. toutes en URSS) étaient parmi les plus grands centres juifs de l'Europe pendant les 18e et 19e siècles, créant une culture très développée. La partie Nord-Est de la Hongrie actuelle avait son propre style, influencé par ces grands centres. Les vieilles écoles célèbres de Bodrogkeresztur ou de Sátoraljaujhely ont joué un rôle essentiel dans la culture juive du pays. Elles avaient des relations avec les communautés de la Grande Plaine Hongroise et en même temps avec la Galicie. Quant à la Transylvanie, des nationalités très diverses s'y sont rencontrées, et la religion juive était pratiquée par des populations de langues allemande, hongroise et roumaine.

Les territoires des dialectes musicaux n'ont que des frontières vagues. Les *hazzanim*[1] étaient toujours en voyage entre les communautés, quelques-uns d'entre eux ne se fixaient jamais. Les gens simples ne restaient pas non plus chez eux toute leur vie, mais visitaient les célèbres *yechivoth* et les grands rabbins même à l'etranger. Quoi qu'on puisse distinguer nettement les

---

*   Publié en hongrois: Zenetudományi Dolgozatok 1980, p. 139–58.

1.   N'importe quel membre de la communauté peut exercer les fonctions l'officiant, les fidèles s'en chargent à tour de rôle, d'où le nom hébreu de l'officiant: *cheliaḥ tzibour* (délégué de la communauté). Chargé originalement de devoirs divers pour la synagogue, le *ḥazzan* assumait les fonctions de l'officiant dès les 6e–7e siècles. Plus tard, le nom *ḥazzan* s'appliquait aux officiants les plus doués pour l'improvisation et pour la voix. Le nom de *cantor* (chantre) était probablement emprunté à l'Eglise au cours du 18e siècle. En Hongrie, il y a une confusion dans l'utilisation de ces trois termes. Nous distinguerons entre l'officiant et le *ḥazzan*, ce dernier représentant un niveau musical professionnel. Le nom de *cantor* est réservé aux officiants de la synagogue réformée, qui ont presque toujours une formation musicale acquise dans un conservatoire.

dialectes les plus caractéristiques de Hongrie, il faut donc toujours tenir compte de la possibilité des influences entre les régions différentes, influences dues aux fréquentes migrations des Juifs.

Les enregistrements réalisés jusqu'à présent n'offrent qu'une indication très approximative des dialectes mentionnés ci-dessus. Le travail n'est, aujourd'hui, qu'à ses débuts. Il faudrait des enregistrements bien plus nombreux pour tracer, d'une façon précise, les lignes de la tradition en Hongrie, et ensuite, peut-être aussi celle de toute l'Europe de l'Est.[2]

En dehors de l'étude des différences dialectales, il s'agit également d'examiner le style lui-même, ainsi que d'entreprendre une classification des mélodies. Jusqu'ici, notre recherche s'est limitée à l'analyse des mélodies récitées, et le présent article est la première tentative d'une approche des chants mesurés.[3]

La Stratification de la Musique

La musique religieuse juive comprend deux styles principaux: le récitatif et les chants mesurés. C'est le premier qui a conservé le plus d'eléments anciens; on peut y retrouver le principe de "mode" au sens oriental du terme, et beaucoup de mélodies appartiennent à l'ancienne culture monophonique de la Méditerranée et de l'Europe du Moyen Age. Le récitatif, souvent élaboré d'une manière mélodieuse et riche, est la manifestation musicale la plus naturelle de la communauté, il est indispensable pour la prière. La mélodie récitée fait partie de la prière et de la tradition, conservée de génération en génération.

Un chant mesuré, par contre, peut changer, être remplacé par un autre chant de composition nouvelle. Il y a de nombreux chants archaïques entre eux, mais on ne les considère pas pour autant comme une partie constante de la tradition. Un bon ḥazzan connaît plusieurs mélodies pour le même texte et ne chante pas toujours la même version. Les chants mesurés ne se présentent que dans quelques sections déterminées de l'office synagogal. La musique du foyer, elle, comporte pour la plupart des chants mesurés, appelés *zemiroth* (d'après la prononciation courante en Hongrie, *zmirès*).[4]

2. Nous tenons à remercier M. Zoltán Simon qui nous a fait part de ses observations sur les dialectes musicaux de Hongrie.
3. Voir: Judit Frigyesi et Péter Laki: "Free-Form Recitative and Strophic Structure in the Hallel Psalms". *Orbis Musicae* 7 (1979/80) 43–80.
4. Appartenant à la tradition achkénaze, la prononciation de nos informateurs est très variable. Malgré certains caractères communs, on peut observer de nombreuses variations. Par la suite, nous allons donner les prononciations hongroises des mots utilisés dans le texte, quand elles diffèrent de la forme sépharade, sous laquelle les mots hébreux sont cités dans le texte. Le mot *zemiroth* signifie 'chant, hymne'.

On pourrait affirmer que le récitatif est toujours plus ancien et se pratique à la synagogue, tandis que les chants mesurés constituent une couche plus moderne et sont utilisés dans le foyer. Le rapport entre les deux est cependant trop étroit pour qu'on puisse former des groupes séparés. Souvent, il ne s'agit que de différentes manières d'exécution de la même échelle et des mêmes motifs, disposés d'une façon variée dans la même pièce. Un chant récitatif peut toujours contenir une petite section ou une strophe mesurée, et il arrive aussi que les sections en récitatif et les strophes mesurées alternent régulièrement.[5] La prière *'El 'adon*[6] en offre un bon exemple, puisqu'elle est connue avec plusieurs mélodies mesurées et non-mesurées. Une des versions généralement répandues donne une succession de strophes mesurées et non-mesurées, la cinquième étant un récitatif avec l'insertion de quelques mesures bien rythmées. (La pièce est chantée d'une manière remarquable: apres l'insertion rythmique, le tempo du récitatif est retrouvé avec une exactitude parfaite.) (Exemple 1)[7]

5. Le terme "strophe" ne peut être utilisé qu'avec une certaine réserve, étant donné que la plupart des textes sont en prose. Un texte donné est cependant toujours divisé en parties bien proportionnées qui peuvent servir de base à une véritable structure strophique dans la musique.
6. *'El 'adon 'al kol ha-ma'asim* (Dieu est le Seigneur de toutes les creatures), variantes de prononciation: *El odaoun* ou *El odaïne*. C'est une prière de l'office du matin pour samedi, hymne alphabétique (chaque vers commence par une autre lettre de l'alphabet).
7. Les exemples musicaux sont transcrits d'après les enregistrements faits le 28 août 1978 avec M. Jenö Roth, Budapest, Hongrie. Les textes sont translitérés phonétiquement suivant l'orthographe hongroise, en respectant rigoureusement la prononciation de l'informateur. Les syllabes rajoutées par celui-ci sont marquées par des lettres légèrement inclinées.

Exemple 1. (suite)

L'inverse, c'est-à-dire la transformation des unités mesurées en récitatif est une formation tout aussi fréquente à la fin des pièces, pour désigner des cadences de différents niveaux. Dans une autre version de *'El 'adon*, on peut trouver une petite section de récitatif au milieu de la pièce (à la fin de la 3e strophe), tandis que la fin de la pièce elle-même est marquée par une strophe entièrement en récitatif. La transition entre récitatif et mesuré est complètement graduelle, elle ne peut être exprimée même par la notation la plus détaillée (Exemple 2, voir la transition entre les strophes 2 et 3).

On voit donc que les deux styles peuvent bien apparaître dans la même pièce. On ne saurait, par conséquent, les considérer comme des couches tout à fait à part. Il faut souligner qu'en général, c'est le récitatif qui est à la base de toute la vie musicale. Il est utilisé dans les prières dont il caractérise le langage musical. Dans une communauté traditionnaliste, les emprunts faits à l'entourage non-juif s'assimilent très vite, et les compositions nouvelles respectent elles aussi la tradition musicale. Les chants mesurés doivent se conformer aux modes du récitatif. Ce rapport étroit explique qu'une mélodie de danse puisse servir comme prière, ou qu'on entende le style récitatif traditionnel dans des pièces extraliturgiques comme des ballades populaires. Parfois, on y retrouve la mélodie exacte d'une prière connue.

La Construction des Mélodies

On peut toujours parler d'une attitude de compositeur dans les différents genres de la musique juive. Bien que le chant synagogal s'inscrive dans des cadres rigoureusement définis, il n'y a pas de mélodies toutes faites dans la liturgie. L'officiant peut, et doit, improviser, à condition seulement de ne pas

Exemple 2. אל אדון (variante mesurée)

Exemple 2. (suite)

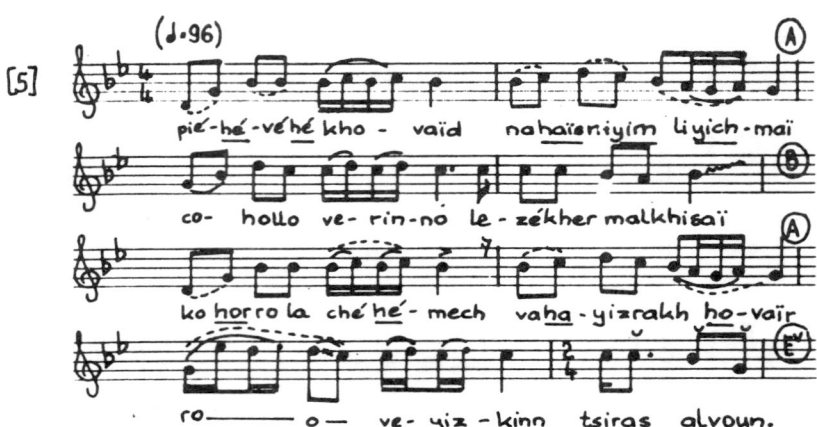

Exemple 2. (suite)

sortir du cadre donné par un certain nombre de formules, un schéma de forme et de mélodie, et un système tonal bien déterminé. L'ensemble de tous ces facteurs est désigne dans la musique arabe par l'expression *maqam* qui a pour équivalent le terme hébreu *nousaḥ*.[8] C'est l'idée générale de la mélodie qui vit dans la conscience du chanteur, et cette idée vient se réaliser sous des formes différentes, grâce aux combinaisons multiples des formules stéréotypes. Ce caractère de la musique juive l'apparente aux cultures musicales orientales.[9]

Dans la musique liturgique, la composition des airs nouveaux n'est pas un acte considéré comme de la composition proprement dite. Néanmoins, les différentes versions de la même pièce présentent parfois des divergences si importantes, qu'il faut bien admettre les styles individuels de certaines régions et de certains officiants (*ḥazanouth*). Les grands *Hazzanim* ont développé un style très personnalisé, évoluant tout au cours de leur vie et se transmettant aux disciples comme un héritage personnel.

8. Le mot *nousaḥ*, dont le sens original est "forme, manière", est devenu un terme musical pour la musique liturgique juive. Variantes de prononciation: *nüsaḥ*, *nisèḥ*.
9. Voir Avenary, H.: "The Concept of Mode in European Synagogue Chant." In: *Yuval 2* (Jerusalem, 1971).

Beaucoup de prières n'ont pas de *nousaḥ* particulier, et la plus grande partie de l'office se déroule dans un récitatif simple à la formule générale. Le choix de chaque communauté dans la distinction de certains extraits est le résultat d'une évolution séculaire. L'officiant et les fidèles peuvent le changer en simplifiant quelques chants ou en faisant ressortir d'autres textes, ce qui est certainememt de la composition suivant des règles du *nousaḥ* traditionnel. L'un de nos informateurs a raconté la naissance de l'une de ses compositions pour la prière *Qedoucha*:[10]

"*A Hanusfalva, où j'ai fait mes études, l'officiant ne s'occupait pas trop de la Qedouchah. Il connaissait beaucoup de belles choses, mais la Qedouchah, il la finissait très vite pour ne pas se fatiguer avant le 'leinen'* (lecture de la Torah) *et tout le reste. Il chantait plusieurs nigounim pendant le même office, dont 'El 'adon, donc c'en aurait déjà été trop. Mais chez nous, on débite maintenant en toute vitesse le 'El 'adon, et le reste n'est tellement fatigant non plus, donc j'ai tâché d'en mettre un tout petit peu dans la Qedouchah au moins. La Qedouchah n'a pas de nousaḥ particulier, d'habitude, on la récite comme les autres prières. Mais pourtant elle est un peu plus que ça, c'est tout de même le centre de toute cette prière, alors, j'ai tâché d'y donner un peu de ma propre personnalité. C'est comme ça que je l'ai composée, cette Qedouchah. Si elle est réussie ou non, c'est aux autres de le dire.*" (Viktor Feuerlicht, 14.4.1980)

La composition du *ḥazzan* n'est pas considérée comme nouvelle, la communauté y entend toujours le *nousaḥ*. Les chants métriques, eux, sont censés apporter une nouveauté. Conservation d'une part et le désir d'innovation de l'autre – voilà la dualité qui caractérise les chants domestiques et aussi les chants mesurés de la synagogue. La plupart des *zemiroth* sont des poèmes religieux du Moyen Age (*piyoutim*), chantés depuis lors sur des airs populaires de l'epoque. Les mélodies sont souvent anonymes, mais il est certain que la population juive des villes et des villages ne manquait jamais de personnes capables d'enrichir le répertoire en composant des mélodies nouvelles sur les textes traditionnels. C'etait le cas particulièrement chez les Hassidim. Chaque rabbi ḥassidique avait son "musicien de cour" qui fournissait les chants pour les grandes fêtes et les repas communautaires du samedi.

Le compositeur et chef de choeur Chemjo Vinaver[11] a encore connu de tels compositeurs. "J'en ai connu un dans ma jeunesse," écrit-il, "c'était Reb

10. *Kedusha* (Sanctification), la révélation de la sainteté de Dieu qui correspond au Sanctus Latin.
11. Chemjo Vinaver (1900–1974), compositeur et chef de choeur né à Varsovie, un des plus grands connaisseurs du chant ḥassidique. Toutes les notation qu'il avait faites dans sa jeunesse étant perdues pendant la guerre, il les nota de mémoire après de longues années, pour sa collection d'une valeur exceptionnelle.

Moché Noah de Lodz. Quand je l'ai rencontré a l'âge de onze ans, il était déjà trés âgé; mais avait toujours l'enthousiasme ardent d'un vieux Ḥassid... Bien que je n'aie passé que peu de temps avec lui, j'ai été profondément touché par l'attention minutieuse avec laquelle il suivait le travail d'un enfant qui notait ses mélodies. Il veillait à ce que les nuances les plus subtiles ne se perdent pas. Je n'oublierai jamais cette sensibilité et cet attachement profond à la musique juive." (Vinaver, 20)

Nous ne savons pas beaucoup sur la vie dans les cours ḥassidiques, et nous connaissons encore moins la manière dont les mélodies étaient composées, puis acceptées (malgré les informations données par Avenary, *Encyclopaedia Judaica* 12: 638). Il n'y a qu'un seul informateur qui nous en ait parlé.

"Je ne sais pas combien il y a de chants nouveaux aujourd'hui, mais de mon temps, quand j'etudiais le Talmud à Szatmár en 36–38, alors là, il y avait des mélodies chaque année qui venaient de différents ḥazzanim, et nous en faisions une sélection pour le rabbi. Le rabbi choisissait là-dessus une quinzaine de mélodies qui nous servaient pour toute l'année. On faisait cette sélection avant les grandes fêtes, en prévoyant une mélodie à chaque occasion pour l'année suivante. On présentait tout au rabbi qui disait: 'Bien, on va utiliser ça comme cholem alékhem.' Alors, on apprenait la mélodie à un choeur de vingt à vingt-quatre garçons, et le compositeur venait nous aider à adapter la mélodie au texte du cholem 'alékhem et comme ça, on avait un chant pour toute l'année. De même, toutes les melodies recevaient un rôle à jouer, et chaque fois qu'on arrivait à tel texte, on commençait à chanter la mélodie convenable." (Viktor Feuerlicht, 14.4.1980)

C'est au rabbi qu'incombe le choix, puisque c'est lui qui sait le mieux juger, quelle mélodie exprime le mieux un texte donné. Les paroles de ce dernier seront appliquées tant bien que mal à la mélodie. En chantant, c'est à la mélodie qu'on se concentre, et on fait souvent comme si le texte n'existait pas. (Il m'est arrivé de voir un chanteur qui savait très bien pour quel texte la mélodie était employée, mais ne se rappelait plus la disposition des paroles.) Le texte est bien entendu très important; mais ce ne sont pas les paroles mais la mélodie qui en exprime le véritable contenu. On connaît un air de Chabath, chanté par toute une cour ḥassidique entièrement sans paroles tout en sachant que le *nigoun* appartient à un texte déterminé (voir Hajdu-Mazor, *Encyclopaedia Judaica* 7:1422).

"Ces mélodies nous venaient de Roumanie ou de Pologne. Le rabbi avait beaucoup d'adeptes dans le monde, et il y en avait bon nombre de chanteurs et de ḥazzanim.. Ceux-là ne faisaient que ça toute l'année. En éte, chacun d'eux envoyait deux ou trois mélodies, destinées pour les grandes fêtes, afin que le rabbi en fasse son choix. Le rabbi avait des spécialistes, des gens qui lisaient la

musique. Et quand le rabbi disait 'eh bien, on prend celle-là,' on faisait venir le poète pour qu'il chante sa mélodie devant le rabbi, et qu'il nous l'enseigne. Des fois, on gardait certains chants pendant plusieurs années, ni le rabbi, ni la communauté ne voulaient les changer, car on ne trouvait pas mieux. Et tant qu'on ne trouvait pas mieux, on utilisait la mélodie qui avait fait ses preuves... On ne changeait jamais le nousaḥ, et on ne se servait d'un nigoun que pour permettre au rabbin, qui était en même temps officiant, de se reposer; et on chantait une mélodie pour que le rabbi puisse se reposer un tout petit peu. Mais on en chantait surtout à la Simḥat Torah, et tous les Chabaths à la table du rabbi." (Viktor Feuerlicht, 14.4.1980)

Le Style des Chants Mesurés

En acceptant une mélodie comme authentiquement ḥassidique, et en l'attribuant à une cour déterminée, les ḥassidim procèdent à partir de critères musicaux et s'expriment à l'aide d'une terminologie musicale traditionnelle, jusqu'ici peu étudiée (voir Hajdu-Mazor, *Encyclopaedia Judaica* 7:1421). Il est évident que tous les *nigounim*, comme d'ailleurs les récitatifs, appartiennent à un style strictement déterminé, les différences qui peuvent se rencontrer n'etant que des variantes dans un certain cadre de la forme, du rythme et de la tonalité. Pour les ḥasidim, cependant, il y a une différence essentielle entre les deux manières de composition. Le *nigoun* n'est pas considéré comme une "mélodie conservée," il est au contraire une "melodie retrouvée," son caractère religieux ne se fonde pas sur le fait de perpétuer un message archaïque sous sa forme traditionnelle, mais sur le fait que, dans lui, et grâce à lui, on a pu accéder à "l'idée divine." Les inventeurs de *nigounim* sont donc appelés des compositeurs ou poètes, tandis qu'on n'applique jamais ces expressions aux *ḥazzanim*.

Quels sont les caractéristiques du style de ces mélodies? Tout d'abord, il convient de noter le rapport étroit entre les chants mesurés et le style récitatif. Ce n'est pas seulement le principe musical qui est semblable, ils offrent aussi des analogies entre les mélodies elles-mêmes. Les notes principales, les cadences et le système tonal sont presque toujours identiques. La structure des motifs et des lignes est aussi bien souvent la même. Dans la prière *'El 'adon*, par exemple, à toute ligne de récitatif correspond une ligne de giusto (Exemple musical 2: X=H ou M, Y=N, P=K ou H, Z=E). Une grande partie des chants mesurés ne sont que des variantes de récitatifs, mais aux contours plus fermes, exprimant le même contenu musical sous une autre forme rythmique.

Il faut supposer, une fois de plus, une conception musicale sous-jacente, semblable au principe du *maqam*. Une série déterminée de notes principales

Exemple 3.

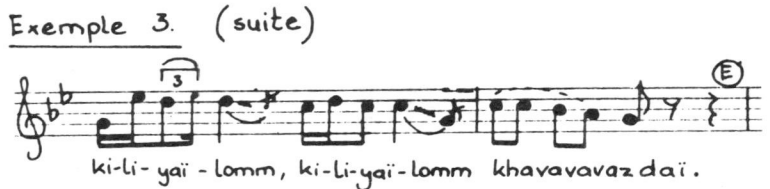

ki-li-yaï-lomm, ki-li-yaï-lomm khavavavaz daï.

d'une part, et la liberté de l'articulation et des proportions intérieures de l'autre, ce sont des phénomènes qui se retrouvent dans la construction des pièces en récitatif, qui, elles, nous l'avons vu, respectent les lois du *nousaḥ*.[12] Les mêmes éléments de base peuvent engendrer des pièces courtes ou longues, mesurées ou non-mesurées, des épisodes intercalés dans une pièce toute différente, ou bien des airs de danse quasiment infinis. En effet, toutes les pièces peuvent être continuées jusqu'à l'infini, ce qui constitue un des caractères principaux des *nigounim* ḥassidiques. Même les morceaux à reprise, qui ont une forme close, sont parfois le point de départ pour une série infinie de variations.

Je cite, à titre d'exemple, une mélodie mesurée de *"Hodou"*[13] et une composition apparentée sur le texte *'El 'adon* (Exemples 3; 2). Les huit lignes différentes de *"Hodou"* peuvent se ramener à une ou deux lignes de base (A variante de D, B variante de C et de H), dont on ne trouve pas moins de 22 variantes dans *'El 'adon* (16 mesurées sur 22). La bonne vingtaine de lignes différentes qui figurent dans les deux mélodies, ne sont, en réalité, que les variantes des trois éléments: des motifs aux cadences respectivement sur la note finale, la tierce mineure et la quarte. Chacun de ces trois types contient plusieurs familles de motifs qui, toutefois, se ressemblent beaucoup (Exemple 4).

Réduite à ces éléments de base, la mélodie qui à l'interprétation paraissait riche et variée, semble être tout à coup d'une maigreur surprenante. Mais son faible est en même temps son fort: la répétition continue produit un effet spécial. Chantés et dansés á la fois, les *nigounim* entraînent les danseurs jusqu'a l'extase grâce à la répétition, qui pourtant, n'est jamais mécanique: elle change constamment par la ré-interprétation un peu transformée de l'idée principale. Dans cette série de répétitions, même les petites nuances mélodiques ou rythmiques prennent du sens, un véritable Ḥassid ayant soin des détails les plus fins, comme nous l'a montré le passage cité de Vinaver.

12. Pour les observations concernant le récitatif, voir Frigyesi – Laki: *op. cit.*
13. *Hodu la-adonai ki tov* (Rendez grâces au Seigneur car Il est bon): le commencement du psaume 118, partie de la prière Hallél.

Exemple 4.

Ce serait pourtant une simplification erronée que de considérer ces mélodies comme des structures primitives, pareilles à des dictons ou des chants enfantins. La répétition des motifs, loin d'être fortuite, obéit à une structure architectonique bien établie. Le contenu musical des différents motifs est projeté sur les échelons plus élevés, et l'on retrouve, parmi les lignes mélodiques, les mêmes types qu'on a remarqués au niveau des motifs. Une ligne n'est autre chose que l'étalement d'un motif dans le temps; on peut trouver un motif correspondant à chaque ligne et en condensant le contenu musical. Le même rapport existe au niveau des lignes et des paires de lignes, voire à celui des paires de lignes et de la strophe (Ex. 5). C'est un phénomène analogue à celui observé dans la musique classique occidentale, où les différents niveaux des fonctions harmoniques se superposent pour former une série qui va de la simple période jusqu'au schéma fonctionnel des grandes formes.

La forme définitive des pièces, même des plus compliquées, peut toujours être ramenée à la structure en paires de lignes, tout comme chez les mélodies en récitatif. Chaque ligne consiste en un antécédent et en un conséquent, et chaque motif assume l'une ou l'autre de ces deux fonctions formelles. Les

paires de lignes peuvent s'enchaîner jusqu'à l'infini, et cette structure permet au *nigoun* d'être toujours ouvert et de se tisser en toute liberté. En même temps, elle peut se développer vers un système strophique en fixant les degrés musicaux cadentiels pour les antécédents et les conséquents (4, b3;q). Une grande forme architectonique peut résulter soit de la reprise d'une section entière (B), soit de la mise en relief de la troisième partie par une construction différent des paires de lignes ($f - f^v$, $g - g^v$), soit du jeu des cadences de valeurs différente (q^{b3}, q^1, q^{b3-4}) (Exemple 6).

Exemple 6. Schéma formel de "Haïdi"

	motifs et cadences		lignes	strophes
	antécédent	conséquent		
[1]	a ♭3 b 4	p 1 q ♭3	A B	A
[2]	c 4 d ♭3 e 4	r ♭3 p 1 q 1	C D E	B
[3]	f 4 g 4 h 4	f ♭3 g 5 q ♭3-4	F G H	C
[4]	c 4 d ♭3 e 4	r ♭3 p 1 q 1	C D E	B

L'articulation de la grande forme est marquée par des finesses à peine sensibles de correspondances et de réminiscences; la deuxième partie commence par un rappel modifié de la ligne précédente (mêmes cadences, mouvement mélodique différent), et la partie centrale apporte une nouveauté rythmique.

A tout ceci viennent s'ajouter les différences de l'interprétation, les particularités de l'ornementation et du timbre, les changements du tempo et la mise en place des paroles. C'est le style particulier de l'exécution qui rend à ces chants, paraissant banaux au premier abord, toute leur originalité. C'est la façon de chanter qui rend un chant vraiment ḥassidique, et elle contribue beaucoup à sa forme définitive. Le caractère intense du chant montre des valeurs bien supérieures à celles qu'on décèle par l'analyse des partitions. Malheureusement, il devient de plus en plus difficile de trouver un informateur capable d'en évoquer la vraie atmosphère. Aussi n'existe-t-il aucune étude sur la manière de l'interprétation, alors que c'est peut-être là même qu'on arrive le mieux à définir la spécificité de cette musique.

La musique hassidique exerça une influence colossale dans le monde juif; même les adversaires de leur idéologie ne purent s'empêcher d'adopter les mélodies et le style musical des Hassidim. Donc, l'examen des *nigounim* permet de saisir le problème central des mélodies mesurées dans la musique juive en général. La manière dont on se sert de ces mélodies est d'un intérêt ethnologique tout particulier. Si, au point de vue purement musical, elles ne valent peut-être pas le répertoire récitatif, elles n'en représentent pas moins un aspect essentiel de la culture musicale du peuple juif.

Childbirth Songs Among Sephardic Jews of Balkan Origin
A Preliminary Study*

Susana Weich-Shahak, *Tel-Aviv*

The folksongs of the Sephardic Jews, whether liturgical, para-liturgical or secular in nature, accompany the individual throughout his entire life: from birth, through marriage, religious and private affairs, until his death.[1] The present study will examine only one category from this large repertoire of songs. Known as *canticas de parida* (songs for the mother of the newborn child),[2] they are sung in the Judeo-Spanish language of *Judezmo (Ladino)*.[3]

The informants for this study – all Sephardic Jews – may be divided into two groups: first, those born in Jerusalem to families which have lived there for generations; and second, immigrants from Greece, Turkey and Bulgaria who arrived in Israel between 1940 and 1950. Although members of the second group settled throughout the country – in Jaffa, Jerusalem and Kibbutz Nir Itzhak – this scattering did not prevent them from preserving their musical heritage, for while the Sephardic songs have begun to lose their functionality – an inevitable result of Israel's heterogenous population – they are still treasured and frequently sung.

The *canticas de parida* were undoubtedly confined to the specific occasions for which they were created and did not often feature at social gatherings where more general themes were preferred. This may account for the fact that the texts of the *canticas de parida* in our recordings are mostly fragmentary. Not many of these songs are still known today – the informants have only a partial knowledge of them – and it is almost impossible to tell

---

* This preliminary study, part of a research program on Sephardic music of the Jewish Music Research Center, in collaboration with the National Sound Archives (NSA), both at the Hebrew University of Jerusalem, is based chiefly on recordings made by the author between 1974 and 1979. These recordings, as well as additional ones by other scholars, form part of the permanent collection of the NSA (see Appendix for a list of *canticas de parida*).

1. See Attias, Moshé, *Romancero sefardí: romanzas y cantes populares en judeo-español*, 2nd ed., Jerusalem, 1961, and the notes accompanying the record *Sephardic Songs From the Balkans*, by the author of this study, produced by the Jewish Music Research Center and the National Sound Archives at the Jewish National and University Library, Hebrew University, Jerusalem, 1980.
2. In this designation of the songs we can see the social recognition accorded a woman giving birth to a son.
3. See Barocas, David B., *A Study On The Meaning Of Ladino, Judezmo And The Spanish Jewish Dialect*, with an introductory essay by Henry V. Besso, "Judeo-Spanish: Its Growth and Decline," *The Sephardic Stolen Lamp*, Tract Number XI, December 1976.

whether the repertoire was always small or whether it was larger and has been partly forgotten in this century.[4]

It is interesting to note that such songs exist only among the Eastern Sephardic Jews (who lived in countries under the Ottoman rule) and are not present in the repertoire of the Western Sephardic groups (such as those from Morocco, Tangier and Gibraltar). Both groups, however, possess a rich storehouse of liturgical songs in Hebrew that are still sung during the circumcision ritual even today.

Among the songs I have collected, as well as among others that are preserved in the National Sound Archives, we find that a recurrent textual theme of the *canticas de parida* is the idea of the circumcision symbolising the tie between the people of Israel and their God, as described in the Bible. Two songs tell of Abraham, the first of our forefathers to be circumcised, his birth, his mother and his father Terah.[5] (One of these songs was recorded by an elderly woman born in Turkey and raised in Bulgaria, and the other, by a Jerusalem-born informant.) The first one, sung by Matilda Lazar, known mainly by her nickname Mazal Tov (or, as it is pronounced by the Judeo-Spanish speakers: Mazaltó), is the following:

4. Of the eight songs placed by Attias (*Romancero, op. cit.*) in the same category as the subject of this study, only two and part of a third are known to be among the transcriptions presented here. From these eight songs, presented by Attias again in his "Shirei yoldot miSaloniki" ("Birth songs from Salonica"), '*Edot*' vol. 3–4 (1943), pp.269–77, song No. 3 (*Romancero* No. 123) is similar in part to songs No. 3, 4 and 5 of this study, No. 6 (*Romancero* No.126) has the same text as No. 3, and No. 7 (*Romancero* No. 127) to No. 2. All the other songs mentioned by Attias, which will be cited in connection with No. 6 of this study, seem no longer to be remembered, except Nos. 1 and 2 (*Romancero* Nos. 121 and 122). Further field recordings may hopefully recover them as well. Some songs of this study appear in Elnekave, David, "Sefaradismo: folklore de los sefaradíes de Turquía," *Sefarad*, 24 (1964), p. 133, and also in: Luria, Max, "A study of the Monastir Dialect of Judeo-Spanish," *Revue Hispanique*, 79 (1930), pp. 323–75; *Il Buqueto de Romances, Canticas recogidas... por el librero Biniamin b[en] Iosef*, Istanbul, 5896 (1925–6); Uziel, Baruch, *Ha-folklor shel ha-yehudim ha-sefardim* ("The Folklore of the Sephardic Jews"), *Reshumoth*, vol. 6 (1920), pp. 359–97; Brochov, Moshé ben Meshiah, *Ahava we-koz bah* ("Love With a Thorn"), Jerusalem, 1950, p.74; Galante, Abraham, *Histoire des Juifs d'Anatolie – Les Juifs d'Izmir* (Smyrne), Istamboul, 1937, pp. 348–9; Molho, Michael, *Usos y costumbres de los sefardíes de Salonica*, Madrid-Barcelona, 1950 (Biblioteca Hebraicoespanola, III), p. 77; Alvar, Manuel, *Poesia tradicional de los judios españoles*, Ed. Porro a, SA., Mexico 1966 (pp. 28, 29, 180–1).

5. The text resembles the description of the circumstances surrounding the birth of Jesus and of Moses, and is probably based on *Sefer hayashar*, Berlin, 1923, *Parashat Noah* (weekly Bible portion).

Example No. 1

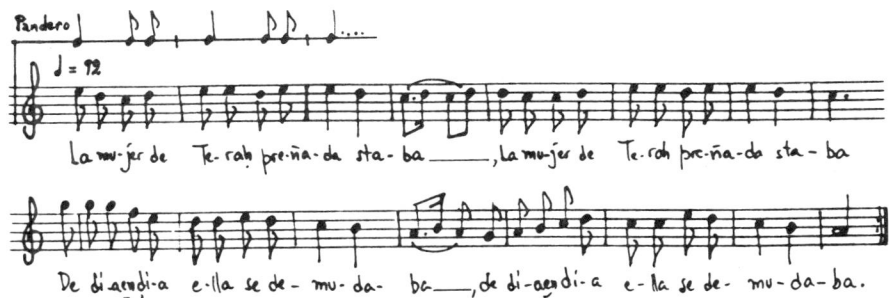

*La mujer de Terah preñada staba
de día en día ella se demudaba.*

*Ni ella no sabía cualo quería
salía por laś calleś como a pedrida.*

*ḍoloreś tenía, parir quería
dónde lo pariera? en la miará,
meldando y ścribiendo en la ishivá.*

*Buen źajú tuviteś señor parido,
que afirmateś la firma de Abram avinu.*

Terah's wife was pregnant,
Each day she grew more pale.

She didn't even know what she wanted,
She wandered the streets like a lost soul.

She had pains, she wanted to give birth.
Where would she have her child? in the cavern? (*m'arah*)
He was studying and writing in the *Yeshiva*.[6]

You had a good *s'chuth*,[7] father of the child,
That you signed *Abraham avinu's* name.

The second song, on the same theme, was recorded by Mordecai Abramov, a Jerusalemite now residing in Tel Aviv. He is well known among Sephardic Jews from Turkey.

6. *Ishivá (Yeshiva)*: institution where the Bible and Talmud were (and are) studied. This allusion to the *ishivá* seems out of historical context, and could be a reference to Jewish daily life at the time and place where this text originated.
7. *zajú*: Sephardi pronunciation of the Hebrew word *z'hut* (privilege).

Example No.2

Cuando el rey Nimrod al campo salía,
miraba en el ciel y en laś estrería
vido luź santa de la judería,
qu'había de naćer Abraham avinu.

Abraham avinu, padre quirido,
padre bindicho, luź de Israel.

La mujer di Terah quedó priñada,
de día en día él la preguntaba:
de qué teneŝ la cara tan demudada?
ella ya sabía el bien que tenía.

When the king Nimrod went out to the field
he looked at the sky and the stars,
He saw a holy light from the Juderia[8]
As Abraham, our father, was about to be born.

Abraham, our father, beloved father,
Blessed father, light of Israel.

Terah's wife was pregnant,
Day after day he would ask her
Why is your face so pale?
She already knew the goodness she was bearing.

The family's concern for the well-being of the mother and her newly-born child is especially marked during the week between the birth and the circumcision. According to popular belief, since mother and child are exposed to the evil eye and other omens during this period,[9] they are never left by themselves, particularly not on the night preceding the circumcision. Both mother and child are attended by the wife's and husband's mothers, who remain with them the entire night, singing to keep awake. In Salonica this night is called *noche de viola* ("wake"). Early during the night the family gathers and various songs, including the *canticas de parida*,[10] are sung by the women present on such occasions.

Another theme of the *canticas de parida* relates to what actually happens, describing the birth and everyone connected with the event; the mother in

---

8. *judería*: the Jewish quarter.
9. See Molho, Michael, *Leida ve-yaldut bein yehudai Saloniki* ("Birth and Childhood Among Salonican Jews"), *'Edoth*, Vol. 3–4, 1943, pp.255–69.
10. *Ibid*, p. 260.

labor, the midwife giving her advice, the family rejoicing with the new male member of the family. It also describes the party, the food prepared for the guests and the parents of the newborn child, with the symbols of wealth and reproduction: coins, fish, candles and fruits.

The third song belongs to this category and can be found in the NSA in various recordings.[11] The following version was recorded by the author as sung by an immigrant from Salonica, Haim Sassa, now living in Kibbutz Nir Itzhak:

Example No. 3

Oh, qué mueve meśeś travateś d'estrechura,
voś nació un hijo de cara de luna,
viva la parida con su creatura.

Ya eś, ya eś buen simán d'ésta alegría,
Bendicho el que moś allegó a ver este día.

Cuando la cumadre diće: dale, dale,
diće la parida: Ah, Dió, escapadme,
diće la su ǵente: Amen, amen, amen.
Ya eś, ya eś...

Ya viene el parido con los convidadoś,
ya trae en la mano cinta y buen peścado,
y en la otra mano resta de ducados.
Ya eś, ya eś.

11. There are many versions of this song, No. 10, recorded in Israel, Greece, Turkey by Amnon Shiloah and Leo Levy, as well as by the author of this study. The version chosen here seems to be one of the more complete in text and clarity of the music (see the recording mentioned in Note 1, above).

Oh, nine months you were in distress,
a son was born to you, his face, beautiful as the moon,
long live the mother and her infant.

It is, it is already a good sign of joy.
Blessed who let us come to see this day.
When the midwife said; go on, go!
the mother says: Ah, God save me,
the family says: Amen, amen, amen.
It is, it is...

Here comes the father of the baby with his guests,
he brings in one hand meat and good fish,
and in the other hand, a handful of ducats (coins)
It is, it is...

The following song is similar, both textually and musically, to the preceding one (see the analysis below), and is also to be found in the NSA in several versions, all of them from Bulgarian Sephardic Jews. The song is presented in two of these:[12] once as sung by Matilda Lazar (Ex. No. 4) and the other by Miriam Conforti (Ex. No. 5), both from Bulgaria.

Example No. 4

12. We present both versions to corroborate the appearance of the refrain and the consistency of the song's form, as will be explained below in its analysis.

Parida, el Dió voś guadre,
cuanto quere la vuestra madre,
parida soś,
parida staba la reina,
paria soś.

Ya viene el parido con laś manoś llenas
en la una mano manźanaś y peraś,
y en la otra mano, llena de candelas.

– Qué hacéś, parida, qué hacéś, mi alma?
S'aqueja la parida que no comió nada,
se come la gallina, los güesos debajo la cama.

Alabar que moś escapó
y este nacido,
sea un buen simán
y este nacido,
también el parido.

Mother of the newborn child, God shall watch over you,
How much your mother wanted you to be the mother of a newborn child.
The queen has given birth,
You are the mother of a newborn child.

Here comes the father of the baby and his guests,
In one hand, apples and pears,
And in the other, a handful of candles.

What do you do, mother of the baby, what do you do, my soul?
The mother complains that she has eaten nothing
Let her eat the hen and leave the bones under her bed.[13]

Let us praise Him who delivered us,
And this newborn child,
Let it be a good omen for this newborn child and
Also for his father.

Example No. 5

Parida, el Dió voś guadre,
cualo quiere la vuestra madre,
parida soś.

13. This is probably also against the evil eye.

*Cuando la cumadre diće: aide, aide,
arisponda la parida: Adonai m'escape.*

*Vino bollido,
bien arevenido,
moś viva'l parido,
también el nacido.*

*S'aqueja la parida que no comió nada,
si coma la gallina, los huesos al bib de la cama.*[14]

*Alabar que moś escapó
a ver ésta alegría,
que seiga un buen simán
y este nacido
que yiva el parido.*

*Avolta, la parida, de cara a la cućina
vireś guiśanderas guiśando comida.
Alabar...*

14.   *arevenido*: arrived? (the meaning is unclear).

Honrad a la **sandaka**, *que todo'l bien merece*
le nació un hijo, que'l Dió se lo presente.
Alabar...

Mother of the newborn child, God shall guard you,
For as your mother wished
You are the mother of a newborn child.

When the midwife says: Go on, go on!
The woman in labor answers: God deliver me!

Boiled wine,
Well received,
Long live the father of the child
And the baby too.

The mother complains that she has eaten nothing,
She'll eat the hen, leaving the bones beside her bed.

Let us praise Him who saved us
To see this joy,
Let it be a good omen for
This newborn child.
Long live the father of the child.

Turn your face towards the kitchen, mother of the newborn child,
You will see women cooking there, cooking for you
Let us praise...

Honor the godmother, she deserves all the best,
She now has a son, let God present him[15]
Let us praise...

Among the Sephardic Jews of Jerusalem, we recorded a *romanza*[16] that was sung in the wake-night preceding the circumcision, usually by an elderly woman. The text of this *romanza* recalls a queen who is about to give birth and longs for her father's castle and for her mother's aid. It will be presented

15. *presente*: could be understood as a corruption of *preserve*, meaning, as in English, that God shall preserve and guard the baby.
16. The use of *romanzas* in connection with events in the life cycle has been discussed in the notes accompanying the record cited in Note 1 (A4). Also, the *romanza* presented in this study does not mention Jewish life but is simply related to the situation fo a woman preparing to give birth (a thematic association).

in the only version that we possess at the NSA, sung by Rivka Shalom, who lives in Mazkereth Moshe, an old quarter of Jerusalem.

Example No. 6

*Dulores tiene la reina,
non los puede senportares*

*quién estuviera pariendo
i en el saray del rey, mi padre.*

*Quién tuviera por većina
a la reina la mi madre,
que me demande piadadeś
la hora que m'echo a parire.*

The queen has pains
She cannot stand them
She would rather be giving birth
In the castle of her father, the king,

Where she could have as her neighbor
Her mother the queen
Who would pray for me
When I begin my labor pains.

While there is no actual evidence that the last song of this study (sung by Dona Purgador, of Bulgarian origin),[17] which was not recorded by the author, belongs to the *canticas de parida*, or that it was sung in connection with circumcision, it is nevertheless included as it closely resembles some songs transcribed by Moshe Attias.[18] He clearly connects them with *la viola*, the night of watching before the circumcision, in which the husband's mother reminds her daughter-in-law how she raised her son, asking the cock to sing to announce the coming of day and the ceremony it brings.

Example No. 7

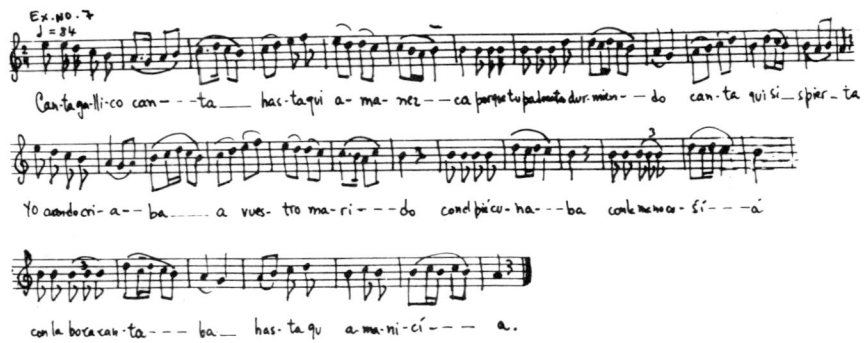

*Canta, gallico, canta
hasta qui amanežca
purque tu padri stá durmiendo
canta qui spierta.*

*Yo cuando criaba
a vuestru marido
con el pié cunaba
cun la manu cuśía,
cun la boca cantaba
hasta qui amanićía.*

Sing, little cock, sing,
until morning comes,
because your father is sleeping,
sing, so that he should awake.

17. From the town of Shumen, from which, unfortunately, we have no other recordings.
18. In the *Romancero*, songs Nos. 121 and 122, which also appear in his *Shirei yoldot misaloniki* as Nos. 1 and 2 c (a, b).

When I nursed
your husband,
with the foot I rocked the cradle,
with the hand I sewed,
with the mouth I sang
until the morning came.

Musical Characteristics of the Sephardic Birth Songs

1. Rhythm

The *canticas de parida* presented here are mostly in duple meter, except the first stanzas of songs Nos. 4 and 5, which are in triple meter (we will refer to this feature below, under the parameter of *Form*).

All the songs, with the exception of the *romanza* (No. 6), are accompanied in performance by the *pandero* (or *panderico*), a round drum or tambourine generally played by women. The accompanying rhythmic pattern of the *panderico* consists of one quarter and two eighths [♩ ♫] or subdivided as [♬♬♫].¹⁹

In all the songs the beat is clear, except, again, for the *romanza*, whose rhythm is free, almost rubato, with many melismas and fermatas. In Nos. 3 and 4 (A and B) there is a marked similarity between the meter and the words of the identical lines, as is shown in Example No. 8. There is also a correspondence between accented or stressed beats and common notes, as in bars 2 (E and D), 4 (D and B, with an upper added note in song No. 4), bar 5 (C and D), bar 6 (E), bar 7 (G and F) and bar B (E).

Example No. 8: Comparison of songs Nos. 3 and 4/5

19. Some of the versions used are sung without accompaniment of the *pandericos*; the notation of the accompaniment is, however, given as it appears in other versions of the same informants that were not as complete from a textual and musical (formal) point of view. *Cf.* songs Nos. 1, 2 and 3 on side B of the above-mentioned record, corresponding, respectively, to songs Nos. 1, 3 and 4 of this study.

2. Melody

All these songs have quite a wide range, extending to a seventh, octave or ninth. The melodies are mainly conjunct, moving mostly by seconds, interspersed with occasional thirds, fourths and fifths. In song No. 3, from Greece (and also in the Turkish versions in the NSA) a skip of a seventh appears towards the end. This interval, which might simply occur as a way of preventing too low a tessitura, may also be a kind of intensification of embellishment[20] (see song No. 3, bars 30 and 39).

The melodic motion is also primarily descending. This has been measured by their Directional Index[21] which is less than 1 in all the songs; only No. 6 is 1 (see the exact numbers in Note 21).

The songs are chiefly in minor modes, with the exception of No. 2, which, with its minor second and major third above the finalis is what is known in the East as close to the *maqám Hidjaz*, and among Ashkenazi Jews as the *shteiger* called *Ahavá raba*. Songs No. 1, 5 and 6 are in the A mode and Nos. 3 and 4 in the E. An exception is the first stanza of No. 4, both in its A and B versions, in what is generally called C major. We shall refer to this in discussing *Form*.

In all these songs we can point to the appearance of a subfinalis or subtonic note, a major second below the finalis: in the A mode it is G, in E it is D. This subfinalis usually appears near the end of the musical phrase. Two exceptions to this are song No. 2, whose range does not extend below the finalis, and the first musical stanza of No. 4 (A and B). This subfinalis note may also be found in other examples of the Sephardic musical heritage, including wedding songs and *romanzas*.[22]

The subfinalis seems to belong to a penultimate motive, appearing near the end of the musical stanza, and signalling its closing on the finalis. It consists of a descending melodic line, generally quite short, that is based or ends on the subfinalis (see song No. 1, bar 12; No. 3, bars 20, 27 and 35; No. 4, bars 22, 40 and 44; No. 6, before the end of the stanza; and No. 7, bar 31).

20. See Appendix. This feature of the transposition of a septime which, appears consistently in almost all the versions, near the end of the song (the last bars of the refrain, though not always in the same place) has been explained to me by Prof. A. Shiloah as a way of embellishing the end of the refrain, an explanation for which I am most grateful.
21. The Directional Index, adopted by the Musicology Department of Tel-Aviv University, is a procedure by which the prevailing direction in a melody is calculated by dividing the number of ascending intervals by that of descending intervals (ignoring interval-size as well as repetitions of identical notes). The D. I. of the songs are as follows: No 1: 0.66; No 2: 0.54; No 3: 0.75; No 4: 0.63; No 5: 0.70; No 6: 1; and No 7: 0.74.
22. See the author's article, "The Wedding Songs of the Bulgarian-Sephardi Jews," *Orbis Musicae*, No. 7, Faculty of Arts, Tel-Aviv University, 1979/80, p. 102.

Usually, the subfinalis note is followed by a melodic motion which arrives on the finalis from above (see Ex. No. 9).

Example No. 9: Penultimate motive

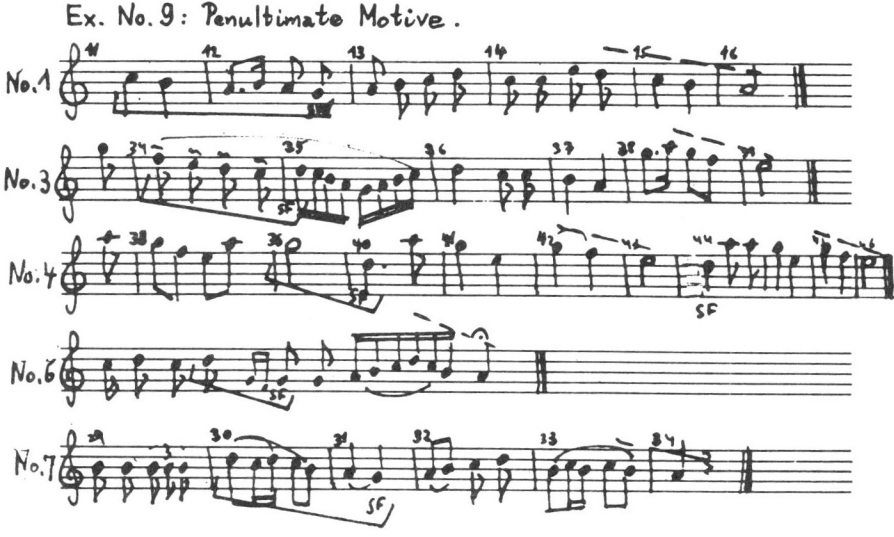

In the A mode songs the subfinalis occurs on an unstressed beat at the end of the penultimate motive or phrase. Nos. 3 and 4, in the E mode, are in the *maqám Huzam*. Here the song usually ends with a melodic motive in which the minor third, on a stressed beat, descends to the finalis. This same feature can be seen also in other songs, not in the *canticas de parida*, but with similar characteristics, *e.g.*, in *Arbolicos de almendra* (see Ex. No. 10).

Example No. 10

3. Form

All the songs relating to circumcision presented here have a strophic form with musical phrasing corresponding to the textual stanzas. Some of the songs also have a refrain (Nos. 2, 3 and 4). In No. 3 each textual stanza contains three lines, paralleled by three melodic phrases in each musical stanza. Songs Nos. 4 and 5 exhibit stanzas of four lines and the musical stanza similarly presents four phrases. No. 6 belongs clearly to the category of *romanzas*, both in its textual features (non-Jewish subject, strophes of 8 syllables in each line, with all even lines in assonant rhyme) and in its musical characteristics (free rhythm, no clear metrical division, unaccompanied performance, strophic form with slight variations).

Both musical and textual material is frequently repeated, as we can see in two of the songs from Bulgaria (Nos. 1 and 4/5). Here the first textual line and the initial musical phrase are sung twice, the tendency to such repetition being also common to Bulgarian wedding songs.[23] Another aspect, also found in some wedding songs,[24] is the appearance of an opening textual stanza sung to one melody, while the remaining stanzas are sung to another. The entire song, therefore, is structured ABBB. This is also found in No. 4/5 (both versions) where the first textual stanza (*"Paride, el Dió vos guadre..."*) is sung to a melody totally different from the following stanzas: its C mode contrasts with the rest, which is in E, and its meter is triple, as against the duple of the other stanzas.

Songs Nos. 3 and 4 are problematic due to their marked similarity. From the textual side they seem to share one archetypical form. Although the texts are not identical, they nevertheless possess similar thematic and semantic content, as is evident from a comparison of their poetical motifs. The refrains in both songs are different, but the texts in both concern praise and joy. The other stanzas are textually alike, with the same themes, motives and identical lines, suggesting a common source to both songs.

Considering the musical aspect, then, it is obvious that the melodies greatly resemble one another. But while their melodic / rhythmic design is similar, that of No. 4 is much more elaborate, both in its ornamentation and melismas.

The above has been noted in the discussion of rhythm (Ex. No. 8), while considering the coincidence of notes on accented beats; where such coincidence is less, as in bars 3 and 4, the melodic contour is still similar. There are, however, two distinct differences between both songs: first, in the repeated parts, serving as a refrain in each song, the musical difference is clear, as they have two totally unlike melodic-rhythmic designs (this despite the similar text, praising the Lord and rejoicing in the happy event); second, the first

---

23.   *Ibid.*, p. 104.
24.   *Ibid.*, pp. 104–5.

stanza of song No. 4 (the A of its ABBB structure) has no counterpart in No. 3, neither textual nor musical.[25]

From this preliminary investigation of the *canticas de parida*, intended by way of introduction and initial presentation, it is apparent that with further field recordings and stylistic analyses, a more penetrating understanding of this repertoire of the Sephardic musical heritage will be achieved.

APPENDIX

List of the recordings of *Canticas de parida* in the National Sound Archives, Jerusalem (NSA), including examples* presented in this study.

Ex. No.	NSA No.	Recording Location	Informant's Name	Informant's Origin	Recorded by
1	Yc936(2)	Yaffo	Lazar, Matilda	Tur., Bulg.	SWS**
	Yc854(23)	Yaffo	Lazar, Matilda	Tur., Bulg.	SWS
	Y2091(2,3)	Yaffo	Lazar, Matilda	Tur., Bulg.	SWS
2	Yc958(12,13)	Bat Yam	Abramov, Mordecai	Jerusalem	SWS
3	Yc1215(9)	Jerusalem	Dassa, Haim	Salonica	SWS
	Y191(2)	Athens	Masarano	Greece	LL
	Yc1096(11)	Tel Aviv	Cides, Ana	Salonica	SWS
	Yc1599(9)	Yaffo	Avigdor, Suzanne	Istanbul	SWS
	Y1090(5)	Istanbul	Toti, Luna	Istanbul	AS
	Y2709(12)	Jerusalem	Shalom, Cohava	Jerusalem	SWS
	Yc528(7)				AS
	Yc279(23)	Larissa	Negrin, Abraham	Larissa	AS
	Yc478(18)	Istanbul	Bicaci, Margueritte	Turkey	AS
	Yc930(3)	Lima, Peru	Levi, Leah	Istanbul	SWS
4/5	Yc854(22)	Yaffo	Lazar, Matilda	Tur., Bulg.	SWS
	Yc936(3)	Yaffo	Lazar, Matilda	Tur., Bulg.	SWS
	Y2091(2)	Yaffo	Lazar, Matilda	Tur., Bulg.	SWS
	Y2093(4)	Yaffo	Cohen, Sarah	Tur., Bulg.	SWS
	Yc1039(22)	Yaffo	Conforti, Miriam	Tur., Bulg.	SWS
6	Y2833(2,3)	Jerusalem	Shalom, Rivka	Jerusalem	SWS
7	Y3296(1)	Jerusalem	Purgador, Dona	Bulg.	MS
	Y3296(2)	Jerusalem	Davidov, Rahel	Bulg.	MS

* Ex. No. 10, not from the *Canticas de parida*, is NSA No. Y2093(2).
** Key: SWS – Susana Weich-Shahak
      LL – Leo Levy   AS – Amnon Shiloah   MS – Moshé Shaúl

25. I would like to thank Prof. Hanoch Avenary and Dr. Uri Sharvit for their advice, patience and encouragement towards the completion of this preliminary study.

RESEARCH REPORTS
The Nāy or Arab Flute*
Yohanan Ron

Introduction

The *nāy* is an end-blown (or rim-blown) flute, common throughout the Islamic countries. Persian in origin, the word *nāy* means "pipe" or "reed". The instrument's ancestors were the end-vibrated flutes used by the Egyptians *circa* 3,000 B.C.E. Since then the *nāy* has had an unbroken history in the Middle East.

End-blown flutes, the *nāy* among them, consist of a single cylindrical tube, of no special material, open at both ends – having, that is, no *embouchure* or mouth-piece. They are common today wherever ancient cultures have been preserved (in Asia, Africa, South America and elsewhere). Most of them are of simple construction, their shape hardly having changed through the ages. They are usually used to play local folk-music.

Tones are produced in an end-blown flute by blowing a stream of air at the mouth-hole such that it impinges on the opposite edge of the hole, thereby vibrating the air column in the tube.

Several types of *nāy* are to be encountered in the countries of the Arab world:

a. the folk-*nāy*, of which there are many versions, is a simple affair, improvised by its owner – player from any suitable material conveniently at hand: natural cane (reed), metal or plastic pipe, *etc.* It is of no fixed dimensions, nor does it have a fixed number of finger-holes. Its range may vary from a fourth to an octave. It is most common in remote villages and among Bedouin tribesmen and shepherds.

b. the north-African *nāy*, sometimes called *shubāba* or *qusaba*, can be quite long, up to 70 or 80 cm. It is made from cane and has six to nine anterior (or upper-side) finger-holes, none on the posterior (or lower) side. Its range can reach a twelfth.

c. the Persian *nāy* (or "nēy") is a piece of cane 50 to 60 cm. long. It has one posterior and five anterior finger-holes. The mouth-hole is encased in metal and the whole instrument is frequently engraved or otherwise decorated. Its range is a twelfth.

d. the *nāy* used for playing oriental art-music (in the urban centres of Arab culture: Baghdad, Cairo, Damascus, Beirut, etc.) is the most advanced type

---
* M.A. Thesis Abstract: Tel-Aviv University, Department of Musicology, 1980.

of nāy and the one treated in this article. Henceforward the term *nāy* refers only to this type, unless stated to the contrary.

Manner of Construction

The *nāy* is made from what is known botanically as the common reed, *phragmites communis*, what most English-speakers would call "cane". That part of the cane chosen must have nine segments, each four to eight cm. long depending on the desired overall length. The shape of the cane is slightly conical, as is the plant in its natural state. The mouth-hole is at the wider, the air exit at the narrower end (*i.e.*, the higher portion of the growing plant is the lower portion of the instrument when held for playing). Seven finger-holes are made, six on the anterior side, one on the posterior, all in the lower or narrower part towards the air exit and away from the mouth-hole. Inside the cane, three to five cm. from the mouth-hole, there is a natural partition or diaphragm blocking the tube in which a narrow orifice is bored (referred to below). The sides of the mouth-hole are finely filed within and without. Smaller *nāys* sometimes have a wooden sleeve surmounted on the mouth-hole; sliding this sleeve forward or backward changes the pitch. In Turkey this cylindrical addition is often of precious stone or ivory. The cane having been cut from the plant, the natural diaphragms which block the tube at each of the segmental joints are removed – save for the one closest to the mouth-hole – and the cane is cleaned inside and out. It is then dried by burying in hot ash. Once dry and clean the orifice is pierced in the remaining diaphragm and the finger-holes are marked and pierced.

The segmental joints serve as coordinates with reference to which the positioning of the finger-holes is determined. First, finger-holes c and d are marked at the two extremities of the third segment, *i.e.*, close to the joints with the second and fourth segments. The exact location of these two holes is a matter of experience on the part of the person constructing the *nāy*; precise measuring aids such as rulers are not used. Moreover, the distance set between these two finger-holes serves as a basis for calculating the location of the other finger-holes. This distance is not constant; it is a function of the *nāy's* size. The next stage, then, is to mark and pierce finger-holes a and f such that the distances a–c, c–d and d–f are all equal. Finally finger-holes b, e and a_1 (the latter on the posterior side) are marked and pierced such that the distances a–b, b–c, d–e and e–f are equal, the distances a_1–b, b–d and c–e are equal, and the distances a_1–a, a–c and d–f are equal.

All the finger-holes and the hole in the internal diaphragm are made using a fine iron poker at white heat. Consequently the holes are neither exactly circular nor identical in size. Once all the holes have been made and the mouth-hole has been filed the *nāy* is tested for tone and intonation. Final adjustment is affected by reducing the *nāy*'s length, *i.e.*, by cutting off small quantities of cane at either of its extremities.

Nāy-type flutes come in different sizes but whatever their size they are all constructed in the manner described above and all have the same basic musical scale. A player will usually own a set of 24 different-sized *nāys* though, as a rule, he will only use several of them. In a particular set measured by the writer, the largest was 760 mm. in length and an outside diameter of 24.5 mm. at the mouth-hole; the smallest was 365 mm. long, the mouth-hole diameter being 15.5 mm. Each *nāy* is lower (or higher) in pitch than the next in size by a quarter of a second.

Examination of the dimensions of various *nāys* reveals that the *proportions* of one are similar to those of any other. It transpires further that the length ratio between different-sized *nāys* is similar to the pitch ratio. For example: a ratio of 1:2 in length gives a difference in pitch of one octave or, in the specific case of the two *nāys* mentioned above, $\frac{365}{760} \simeq \frac{1}{2}$.

Using the dimensions of a *nāy* whose lowest note is d', *viz.*, length approximately 540 mm. and internal diameter approximately 13 mm., in the formula $f = \frac{V}{2L_1}$,
we obtain confirmation that the instrument's proportions are indeed compatible and reasonable:

$$f = \frac{345 \text{ m/sec}}{2 \times 0.558} = \frac{345}{1.116} = 309 = d^1 +$$

It follows that the dimensions of different-sized *naȳs*, taken as ratios, are (more-or-less) equivalent to the acoustic relationships between them. But since the *nāy* is not constructed using precision measurement techniques, it is not possible to fix an instrument's pitch solely on the basis of its physical dimensions.

The Mouth-Hole

End-blown flutes may be categorized according to the characteristics of their mouth-holes. Thus, one category is that in which the mouth-hole is at right-angles to the axis of the tube, another that in which the mouth-hole is at 30°–45° to the axis, yet another that with a notch in one side of the mouth-hole (the *quena*), etc. All these categories, however, have one thing in common: the tube is open along the whole of its length and contains no obstacle to the passage of the air from the mouth-hole to the exit.

In contrast, the *nāy* does contain such an obstacle in the shape of the pierced diaphragm situated 3 to 5 cm. from the mouth-hole. When the *nāy* is played, the air column inside it is not unbroken. The air introduced at the mouth-hole fills the smaller chamber and is then forced through the orifice in the diaphragm. This unique characteristic gives the *nāy* a certain advantage over other end-blown flutes with regard to its tone-producing capacity: it has a wider compass of notes, produces a clean, "tuned" tone, and also produces this series of overtones without any assistance from the fingers:

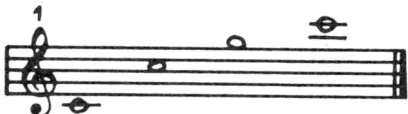

The use of over-blowing to produce overtones enables the flautist to play identical notes in different registers. The shape of the mouthhole in no way affects the absolute pitch.

The shape of the mouth-hole and cavity beyond is similar to that of the *embouchure* of any brass wind instrument (French horn, trumpet, etc.), *i.e.*, it is like a cup pierced at its lowest point. But while in brass instruments a tone is created by vibration of the lips, in the *nāy* the air column is set vibrating by impingement of the air from the mouth on the rim of the mouth-hole. In both cases the "cup" or "funnel" acts as a receptacle in which the air, on its way to becoming a vibrating column, is collected. In both cases, moreover, the air is forced from the "cup" into the vibrating column through a narrow orifice. It appears, therefore, that the similarity in form of the mouth-hole and cavity of the *nāy* and the mouth-piece of a brass instrument would account for the tone qualities of the *nāy*.

Range, Scale, Fingering and Musical Qualities.

The range, or compass, of the *nāy* is two octaves and a fourth. Almost every pitch lying within this range can be produced, including half-tones, quarter-tones and microtones. The basic scale, for all sizes of *nāy*, is that of the *maqām rāst*:

but the *nāy* is not restricted to this scale; almost any other scale or *maqām* can be played on it.

Analysis of the *nay's* natural scale using a melograph did indeed show the basic scale to be the *rāst*. But the melograph also proved that every *nāy* has its own idiosyncratic deviations from the basic pattern, a fact which explains why two *nāys* are never used in one ensemble. It may further be noted that a skilled *nāy* player can produce parallel octaves.

While being played the *nāy* is held at an angle of 20°–30° to the right side of the body, the left hand being above, the right hand below it, as is customary with most woodwinds. The mouth-hole is kept outside the mouth, resting on the lips which are pursed and rounded. In this position the air stream from the player's mouth breaks on the opposite rims, only part of it therefore entering the tube and creating sound.

The Nāy in the Oriental Ensemble

The *nāy* is to be found incorporated in all the instrumental ensembles customary in the Islamic countries: in the nuclear unit of two instruments, drum and flute; in the traditional five-member oriental ensemble consisting of *qānūn*, *'ud*, violin (or *kamancha*), drum and *nāy*; and in the larger orchestral ensembles which in recent years have become familiar in the larger Arab cultural centres such as Cairo, Damascus and Beirut (in addition to the traditional five instruments, they contain violins, cellos and other occidental instruments). In all these ensembles the *nāy* is treated as a solo instrument, especially when the *taḥmīla* is performed. The latter is a kind of song with verse and refrain, the refrain being played by all the instruments together, the verses by the soloist. The refrain is interpreted as an improvisation on the particular *maqām* being used, each player being given the opportunity to demonstrate his virtuosity and the versatility of his instrument. The *nāy*, in addition to its solo passages, participates in the tutti and accompanies the singers, if any.

Thus the place of the *nāy* in the instrumental music of the Orient has always been assured in all ensembles from the smallest to the largest. In the smaller, more intimate ensembles the *nāy* is the sole wind instrument and its effect on the tonal colour and general sound is therefore most pronounced.

The status of the *nāy* player in modern society is similar to that of any other musician in a professional orchestra. In traditional societies, especially among the Dervish in Turkey, he and his instrument enjoy a position of greatest esteem. Muslims generally have always held the *nāy* in respect, apparently because the direct manner in which the player blows into it – the absence of any "mediating" mechanism – suggested to them a close parallel to singing. This, too, probably explains why the *nāy* is used in religious ceremonies and how it found its way into the ensembles that perform art-music.

Robert Schumann's Concept of Music Education*
Lia Laor

Only on very rare occasions does one encounter a composer who declares his pedagogical Weltanschauung; more exceptional is the case of a composer who publishes a monograph in which he explicitly discusses his concepts of music education; but even more unusual is the combination of pedagogical instructions and educational suggestions which are openly directed to the young piano student, especially when attached to a collection of pedagogical piano pieces for children. This study is focused on one of the earliest modern combinations of this type, namely, Schumann's *Album for the Young*, op. 68, and his *Aphorisms*. The questions discussed are: (1) What was Schumann's pedagogical Weltanschauung and was it successfully implemented in the *Album for the Young*? (2) Were Schumann's pedagogical views and piano pieces for children revolutionary, and if so, how did they influence music education in his time?

Schumann's work is evaluated against the background of the works and the various approaches of his predecessors in the field of music education – especially those who wrote piano pieces for children. Two main different approaches might be identified in the field of music education in the end of the 18th century and the beginning of the 19th century: mechanism and holism. Mechanists, like Bertini and Czerny, usually recommend technical exercises as a *sine qua non* for the development of musical interpretative ability, while holists, like C.P.E. Bach, D.G. Türk and M. Clementi, usually emphasize the importance of the interpretative activity for the development of proper technical abilities. The classical paradigm of mechanists is the etude, and that of holists is the character-piece. Most of the piano pieces which had been written for children before Schumann's *Album* was published are definitely mechanistic (except for Türk's and Clementi's works). Schumann himself, aspiring to virtuosity, abruptly ended his pianistic career due to a personal tragedy: as is well known, he hurt his finger while exercising mechanistically. This accident might have been the reason for the decision to devote himself to composition as well as for his views concerning music education.

Schumann's *Aphorisms* reveal a holistic Weltanschauung in the field of education at large and music education in particular. The child is perceived as an autonomous musician from the very start of his music studies and the development of his musical conceptions is established as the ultimate goal in the pursuit of his music education. Thus, the child's technical training is

* M.A. Thesis Abstract: Tel-Aviv University, Department of Musicology, 1980.

always subordinated to the development of his musicality. The *Aphorisms'* recommendations for the child are: develop your imagination and emotional world, and combine this with music theory studies as well as with various musical activities. Moreover, tune your ear and soul. Playing the piano is, according to Schumann, in reciprocal relation to the development of an internalized musical organ.

Was Schumann successful in implementing his concept of music education in his *Album for the Young*? The study shows that the *Album* might be seen as an adequate implementation of Schumann's pedagogical Weltanschauung: it incorporates the means necessary for the child's achievement of musical (intepretative as well as technical) abilities. Schumann's careful treatment of the various elements of composition within the pieces of the *Album* as well as his dynamic and technical instructions, might serve the child in developing his musical capacities. A variety of styles are presented in the *Album*, including some modelled after Bach and others similar to the idiom of his contemporary, Mendelssohn, introducing the child to the world of piano literature. The piano pieces of the *Album* almost always require of the child a highly artistic performance ability. It reflects Schumann's view that playing piano pieces which have no musical value and are artificially assembled for beginners is harmful, or at best useless, for the child's musical education. The child pianist should be engaged, from the very beginning of his career as a musician, in playing and relating only to music which has meaning for him as a child. Indeed, most of the piano pieces of the *Album* are by title and content expressly and directly music for children, no longer mere miniatures but rather small-scale masterpieces.

The publishing of Schumann's *Aphorisms* and *Album* revolutionized the field of musical compositions for young children in Europe in the middle of the 19th century. Many other composers (including Kullak, Heller and Tschaikovsky) published similar albums. Most of them, however, were mere imitations of Schumann's titles, style and sometimes even of his musical motives.

Musimple: Computer-Based Learning of 7-Sign Music Notation System*

Yael Bukspan

MUSIMPLE is a system of musical notation first introduced by the author in 1973. The main objective in developing MUSIMPLE was to make available a notation which would be easy to read and write by hand or by means of any typewriter and readily stored and reproduced in a computer without resorting to special complex programs. In order to meet these criteria the system makes use of a binary notation using the digits 1 and 0 to indicate pitch, and the characters . − = + to indicate rhythm; x signifies a rest.

Experiments have shown that the sheer simplicity of MUSIMPLE notation has made it possible for even dyslectic children to read music easily. The ready adaptability of MUSIMPLE to computers leads to the possibility of connecting a musical keyboard to a terminal in such a manner that the relevant notation will be displayed simultaneously with the operation of the keyboard.

The MUSIMPLE notation is based on the a.m. principle. Its symbols signify the tone-semitone progressions and not each tone per se. The signs 1 0 . − = + were chosen because of their availability on typewriters, printing presses and in all computer languages. The characters 1, a vertical line, and 0, a circle, are easily grasped by children while the characters . − = + have suitable mnemonic characteristics: the smaller signs representing shorter durations and vice versa. The 8–phase cycle of the musical octaves is represented by (((((()) ())))))))))) or by the initials SC, C, G, P, U, D, T, Q (Sub-Contra, Contra, Grande, Piccola, Una, Due, Tre, Quatro). The "inside-out wave-like motion" phenomenon can be recognized visually as left vs. right and is demonstrated by the notation of −

(a) the major scale:

sol	la	si	do	re	mi	fa
0	00	000	1	11	111	1110
			1			
		000		11		
	00			111		
		0	1110			

---

* Presented at the 26th Annual Meeting of The Society for General Systems Research with The American Association for the Advancement of Science, Washington, D.C., January 5–9, 1982. Full text in *Proceedings of the 26th Annual Meeting...*; abstract by permission of The Society for General Systems Research.

and (b) of the complete 12-semitones set:
1   10   11   110   111   1110   1111   0   01   00   001   000, etc.

The work which has been carried out reproducing conventional musical notation will certainly open new vistas in the musical fields of mass printing, storage, research and education. Because of the carefully chosen symbols used in MUSIMPLE, however, complex programs are not required for adaptation to computer storage.

Until now, because of the complexity of conventional music notation, children generally have not been exposed to written music until they have acquired reading and writing skills. The simplicity of the MUSIMPLE notation, however, enables pre-school children to read music quite easily. The results of experiments conducted during 1977/78 (Bukspan, 1979) comparing MUSIMPLE with conventional music notation showed the distinct advantage of the new system in teaching musical literacy to children between the ages of 6 and 9 years. These experiments also showed that the learning of MUSIMPLE bore no correlation with the level of schooling. This led to further experiments which were carried out in 1980 within the framework of special education and which suggested that not only were dyslectic children able to learn MUSIMPLE but that such training in MUSIMPLE might assist them with the acquisition of language literacy. Unfortunately, because of the special conditions and the personal attitudes associated with this special kind of subject, adequate statistical records are not yet available and further experiments are being conducted at the present time.

Madsen's findings (1978) that the positive effect of musical subject matter as reinforcement for learning mathematics at high-school level can be empirically demonstrated, suggest the "power of music" in advancing academic abilities at all levels.

In pilot experiments carried out in 1976 (Kohen-Raz, 1981) it has been shown that the training of disadvantaged and underprivileged children of second elementary grade level with the aid of structured music lessons significantly improved reading abilities in boys and girls who suffered from mild learning disabilities. The lessons consisted of intermodal transfer of visual and auditory cues associated with singing and the playing of simple instruments; the visual cues comprised dots and dashes as well as the projection of slides showing scenes such as a military parade, a seashore or other association with the relevant musical piece being performed. It is suggested that the visual display of the relevant MUSIMPLE notation would be even more effective than unrelated cues such as lines or dots. The conventional notation would not serve this purpose because of the difficulty in immediately recognizing its message due to the similarity of the notes and the complexity of written information.

The author's current objective is to construct an apparatus which connects a keyboard instrument marked with the relevant MUSIMPLE notation to a computer terminal in such a manner as to provide:

1. The simultaneous visual display on the screen of the performed music in MUSIMPLE notation.
2. Simultaneous audio reproduction of music as it is keyed into the computer terminal.
3. Storage, editing and reproduction facilities.
4. Teaching and self-learning facilities with the aid of pre-programmed music lessons.

The MUSIMPLE method may be adapted for communicating other forms of knowledge and could well serve as an initial stepping-stone for the learning of more complex systems.

At the very least, the value of MUSIMPLE lies in its ability to make music literacy accessible to almost everyone, including those who find the conventional complex notation an insurmountable obstacle.

At the best, the author hopes that MUSIMPLE will make its own small contribution towards the promotion of unified knowledge and mutual enrichment of the arts and sciences.

References

Bukspan, Y.
1973 *Towards a New System of Music Notation*. Tel Aviv: International Monograph.

Bukspan, Y.
1979 "Introduction of Musical Literacy to Children by Means of a Binary System of Music Notation: An Experimental Study." *Council for Research in Music Education*. 59: 13–18.

Kohen-Raz, R.
1981 "Postural Control and Learning Disabilities". *Early Child Development*, 20.

Madsen, C.K.
1979 "The Effect of Music Subject Matter as Reinforcement for Correct Mathematics," *Council for Research in Music Education*. 59: 54–59.

FROM THE BOOKSHELF

Karl Erich Grözinger: *Music und Gesang in der Theologie der frühen jüdischen Literatur; Talmud, Midrasch, Mystik.* (= Texte und Studien zum Antiken Judentum 3.) Tübingen (J.C.B. Mohr), 1982. – XIII + 373 pp.

This very useful book is, first of all, a classified and intelligently annotated repertory of texts about music and song in early Jewish sources. However, it is not a book about music in the normal and technical sense; it rather collects the utterances of rabbis and mystical adepts connected with musical concepts during the formative period of Judaism (the first centuries A.D.) – roots of the attitudes towards music that later became traditional.

Music and song are understood by the teachers of the Talmud, Midrash and early mystical writings as a means of communication between man and his creator to no less a degree than prayer, studying the Law, and fulfilment of the ritual and moral commandments. This conclusion of the author (p. 332 seq.) reminds us of a Talmudic account from temple times stating that the sound of music had formed an integral part of the offering ceremony (*qorban*, which means "approaching" the deity: *Jerusalem Talmud*, Eruvin XIII 2; *Babylonian Talmud*, Thaànith 27a and elsewhere). In rabbinic thought, music does not necessarily imply aesthetic values. It is understood neither as sounding reality nor artistic form; but singing and playing before a divine or human ruler rather means a demonstrative act of submission by uttering his praise (p. 336). This must be understood as a continuation of the Biblical "King's jubilation" (*th'ruàth melech*, Deut. 23.11), symbolizing the acknowledgement of royal power by sung acclamations and trumpet-blowing of the people. The ancient Eastern roots of kings' jubilation and fanfares are only hinted at by the author. The reader does not become aware of the fact that they were a common and wide-spread custom with many peoples, and outlived antiquity for a considerable time. The relevant rabbinical doctrine is part and parcel of this general belief; it is transformed, however, according to the specific religious sphere by making song a human obligation before God.

Other relations to ancient Eastern ideas, not sufficiently stressed by the author, are found in the apotropaïc effect of certain sounds such as the rattling of metal (p. 166–170). In the old Babylonian rituals, the sound of copper or the big drum was regarded as the voice of great gods and brought into action against disease and demons. In the Jewish context this conception is regressive but still alive in old women's beliefs (*e.g.*, *Jerusalem Talmud*, Shabath VI 1; 9). The sound of the shofar, however, and the recitation of psalms have preserved their apotropaïc value down to modern folklore. The relations of Jewish musical concepts to the civilized environment remain a little underestimated in Grözinger's study, although their Jewish transformation appears to be an important cognitive means.

A somewhat narrow treatment is applied also to the mystical treatises in which rabbinical concepts of music are rendered grandiosely vivid. Sound and song become a medium of the human encounter with God, acoustical phenomena accompany the highest-possible form of mystical experience, Israel's songs are wound into a crown to the Most High... This section of the book imparts a strong notion of the sublime, music-interlaced absurdities in the visionary mysticism of the early period. Some enlightening specimens of *Hechaloth*-hymns are reproduced in an adequate German translation.

The weakest spot of Grözinger's book is its title. The author himself is well aware of the fact that a systematic "rabbinic theology of music" cannot be expected (p. 4). Therefore, he would have done better to follow his teacher A.M. Goldberg and other scholars whom he quotes, and to speak rather of the image of music and song in early rabbinic and mystical thought (not yet acquiring the definition of "literature"). The author presents the numerous texts in the utmost systematic manner according to theological *topoi*. The reader has to be cautioned to understand this order as a merely technical means of mastering the almost boundless, diversified but nevertheless repetitive material: systematics are not inherent to the tradition itself. However, we have before us a book for study, not for simple reading: it is a valuable mine of information and may well induce, by the impact of its massive material, a desirable clarification of both Judaistic and musicological concepts and opinions.

Hanoch Avenary

Peter Schäfer, ed.: *Synopse zur Hekhalot-Literatur* (=Texte und Studien zum Antiken Judentum 2). XXIV + 299 pp. Tübingen (J.C.B. Mohr), 1981.

The fact that the musical history of late antiquity is deduced mostly from literature is also the cause for reviewing here this modern edition of Jewish esoteric writings from that age. They form a primary source of knowledge for research in Jewish chant – its motivation, its forms, and its place in religious thought. Although all the preserved manuscripts come from the high and late Middle Ages, specialists like the late Gershon Sholem assign the central ideas of these sources to the 1st to 6th centuries A.D.: they belong to the very first period of post-biblical mysticism (*Qabalat haTanaïm*).

However, music research will take interest not only in the factual information, the ideology and the "word-music" of this literature; it is aroused to no less a degree by the methodological considerations of the editor and the originality of his approach which are kindred to certain constellations of ethnomusicological problematics.

Hekhalot literature (*i.e.*, treatises about the firmaments of heaven) shares the idea of a mortal ascending to heaven with certain apocryphical writings, relating to his vision of the upper spheres and their hosts, and his safe return to earth. His state of visionary trance is reached by a technique of autosuggestion that centers in reciting a very peculiar kind of hymns; they form an essential part of these treatises. The "musical" character of their diction has often been pointed out – the immense pleonasm of praise, the exciting power of rhythm ("like the motion of a big fly-wheel" – Sholem), the vowel-harmony: all of them suggesting the technique of inducing hypnosis by repetitive verbal stimulus. We have to imagine these hymns being sung to a varied repetition of melodic phrases, cognate to the suggestive and spell-casting songs all over the world.

The described vision of the heavens abounds in musical experience. It contains ideas that have become universal sources of artistic inspiration: The choirs of angels, their dance around the throne, and the "trump of doom". The *Hekhalot* treatises develop, in legendary form, also ideas about the place of music in the religious culture of Judaism.

The novelty of the present edition by Peter Schäfer and co-workers lies in doing away with the usual, and very inconsistent, division of the material into several quasi-independent and differently titled treatises. The *Hekhalot* texts are rather taken as a continuous stream of (originally oral?) tradition; every manuscript represents a variant selection and wording. Schäfer constructs his edition as a "Heptapla" of seven selected manuscripts representing just as many versions; they appear in seven parallel columns throughout the book. This, nowadays, very peculiar form of editorial presentation is based upon these premises (p. V–VI): the nature of *Hekhalot* literature is a "strongly fluctuating tradition", more distinctly even than with the Midrash and Targum; looking for an *Urtext* would be not only hopeless, but its construction would also be a methodical failure. It is doubtful if there exists something like "a correct version": one variant must not be regarded as "better" or "more appropriate" than the other. Thus the present state of research produces a corpus of traditional texts. It cannot be divided, meanwhile, into primary and later layers (a critical analysis is planned for a later stage).

Several ideas and conclusions of the editor have a familiar ring to the worker in the field of "traditional", orally transmitted music, such as: his saying 'yes' to the pluralism of existence found with anonymous creations; the acknowledgement of fluctuating versions as reality in the sphere of traditions borne by a group and fully absorbed into its life; the futility of looking for an *Urtext* of works which are composed of 'motives'.

In current ethnomusicological research, however, we are accustomed to start with the largest-possible number of variant versions, excluding or reducing, in this manner, the element of individual choice and preferences; we take care to cover the whole territory of the related tradition. In the light of some results achieved by this policy in the musical field, we would have preferred here to see the oriental manuscripts of the *Hekhalot* better represented than by one out of seven and, in general, an increased number of versions. Since Schäfer's 'Heptapla' can hardly be enlarged but its texts are stored in the computer, scanning additional strains of tradition would be a task for data processing. As with music, there exists also a problem of "notation", *i.e.*, stopping the fluctuation of texts by committing them to writing. If, by further analysis, the *Hekhalot* texts could be established as a primarily *oral* tradition, this would be a strong argument for their antiquity. *A propos* the notation: Schäfer's scrupulous transcriptions of the manuscripts reproduce even filler-letters at the end of the lines, and direction words at the bottom of the pages, incorporating them in the text.

Hanoch Avenary

PUBLICATIONS OF THE DEPARTMENT OF MUSICOLOGY
TEL-AVIV UNIVERSITY

DOCUMENTATION AND STUDIES

A series of booklets published by the Department of Musicology in cooperation with the Ch. Rosenberg School of Jewish Studies.

1. Eduard Birnbaum, Jewish Musicians at the Gonzaga Court of Mantua (1542–1628). Revised and updated English edition by Judith Cohen. 52 pp. Facsimiles, Music, Bibliography.

2. Hanoch Avenary, The Ashkenazi Tradition of Biblical Chant between 1500 and 1900: documentation and musical analysis. 88 pp. Facsimiles, Music, Tables, Diagrams.

3. Amnon Shiloah, The Epistle on Music of the Ikhwan al-Safa (Bagdad, 10th century). An annotated translation of the Arabic source. 74 pp. Introduction, Vocabulary.

To be continued   Each number $4.50

EAST AND WEST

1. Hanoch Avenary, Encounters of East and West in Music. Selected writings. 208 pp. Music, Facsimiles, Bibliography. 1980. Price $10.–

2. Edith Gerson-Kiwi, Migrations and Mutations of the Music in East and West. Selected writings. 248 pp. Music, Transcriptions, Bibliography. 1980. Price $10.–

ORBIS MUSICAE
STUDIES IN MUSICOLOGY
No. 8   1982/83

Back-numbers 1–7 available: Price *en bloc* (6 issues) $30.–